Liberty Frye
and the
Sails of Fate

OTHER BOOKS BY J.L. MCCREEDY:

Liberty Frye and the Witches of Hessen (Book One)

The Orphan of Torundi

BOOK TWO

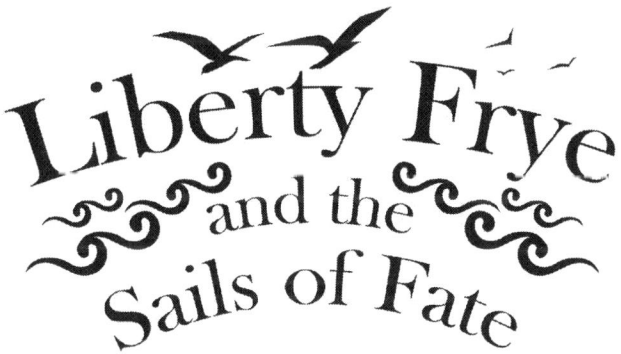

J.L. M^cCREEDY

PENELOPE PIPP PUBLISHING

Copyright © 2016 by J.L. McCreedy
LIBERTY FRYE, characters, names, and distinctive marks are
trademarks of and © J.L. McCreedy. Cover and chapter illustrations
by Cristina Movileanu.
Edited by Karen Carter Communications.

All rights reserved. No part of this book may be reproduced, copied,
stored in any database or retrieval system, distributed or transmitted
in any form or by any means, electronic, mechanical, photocopying,
recording, or otherwise without written permission of the author.

The characters, names, places and events portrayed in this book are
either the product of the author's imagination or are used fictitiously.
Any similarity to real persons, living or deceased, or events is
entirely coincidental.

Published by Penelope Pipp Publishing, McHenry, MS, U.S.A.

www.penelopepipp.com

ISBN-13: 978-0-9882369-4-3/ISBN-10: 0-9882369-4-X (pbk)
ISBN-13: 978-0-9882369-5-0/ISBN-10: 0-9882369-5-8 (e-book)
Library of Congress Control Number: 2015920277

*To Abby, whose enthusiasm for Liberty Frye encouraged me to continue her journey.
And to Sam, for sharing the journey with me.*

Table of Contents

Other books by J.L. McCreedy: iii
Warning. xi
Chapter 1: The Strange Machine 1
Chapter 2: The Terrible Darkness. 10
Chapter 3: Flying Fish 21
Chapter 4: The Atoll Island 31
Chapter 5: The Last Amulet 41
Chapter 6: The Wizard of Qingdao 50
Chapter 7: Storm of Stones 58
Chapter 8: The Visiting Ship 67
Chapter 9: The Substitute Potion 77
Chapter 10: Feathers and Fate 84
Chapter 11: Captain's Quarters 93
Chapter 12: The Disappearance 100
Chapter 13: Gentlemen of Fortune 105
Chapter 14: The Boy in the Shadows 112
Chapter 15: Blackbirding. 118
Chapter 16: Golden Treasure 124
Chapter 17: The Voice from Nowhere 131
Chapter 18: Falling Stars 141

Chapter 19: The Incident.........................153
Chapter 20: Mutiny..............................161
Chapter 21: The Witching Hour 171
Chapter 22: Atamai's Revenge 182
Chapter 23: The Promise 191
Chapter 24: The Severed Curse 197
Chapter 25: Paradise Found.......................205
Chapter 26: Where Time Begins 213
About The Author 223

Warning

It is with a heavy heart that I pen this note. I have tried once before to caution you, but it seems all effort fell vainly at my feet. Nevertheless, I shall endeavor to warn you still.

The account in the following pages is fraught with peril. If you have acquired this tome hoping it is a tale filled with beautiful princesses and prancing ponies, close the cover and walk away. Do not turn around. Do not lift a page.

But if you seek adventure and danger and the dark mysteries of magic, proceed slowly and with great care. You will not be safe. For the mind is a growing labyrinth, churning mere words into ideas, into worlds not bound by sky or ground. You have been warned.

And now, I shall begin the tale.

Chapter 1

The Strange Machine

One hazel eye stared straight ahead. It was all that Libby could see from her position in the backseat of their station wagon.

Her dad simply wouldn't look at her, no matter how many times she glanced at his reflection in the rearview mirror. Libby's mom kept her back to her as well; nothing but a curtain of long, black hair with an increasing shock of white that circled a third of the way around her head now.

"It *is* my birthday, you know," Libby said, breaking the silence. She glanced down at her pet goose, Buttercup, for support. She didn't bother trying Ginny, who sat on the other side of the backseat. Forget about all that best-friend-loyalty stuff; ever since Ginny had moved in with them, she'd been nothing but the world's most perfect foster daughter. "If you won't tell me where we're going, at least we could stop and get Uncle Frank first. It'll hurt his feelings if we don't!"

This was met with a collective shrug of the shoulders from the front seat.

"Libby, I'm sure your parents have a good *reason*," said Ginny.

Libby looked down at Buttercup to hide her irritation. She was beginning to wonder if her newfound powers were actually making her invisible to her parents. Who needed her around when Ginny was so much better? At *everything*. Better at following the rules; better at doing her homework; better at volunteering to do the dishes, even.

Every. Single. Day.

But the worst thing of all was that Ginny was better at being normal … and there was nothing Libby could change about that. Being a witch really stank sometimes. Especially when you don't know what you're supposed to *do* about it.

"And anyway," added Ginny, adjusting her posture so she sat perfectly upright, hands folded in her lap, "you shouldn't be leaning against the window like that since the power button is faulty. Did you know that eighty-eight percent of reported injuries from car windows involve a person's hand or finger getting smashed?"

"Thank you, Ginny," laughed Libby's mom. "I don't know how we ever managed without you!"

Libby took a deep breath, dropped her hand from the rubber trim and then looked out of the window in disgust. Who knew turning eleven could be so depressing?

Outside, the air was already heavy and hot—so heavy it was hard to breathe—and the sky was an ugly, steel grey, like smears of grease from Uncle Frank's shop rags.

Libby squeezed her eyes shut for a moment and took another deep breath. Then she looked down at the little book of spells in her lap, *Das Klein Buch der Magie*, that Sabine had given her just before she'd left Germany. It helped Libby forget about everything else when she studied it. She tried hard to relax her mind, tried to "throw it out of her head," just like the book said to do. But throwing your head *out* of your head isn't as easy as it might sound.

Just relax, the book cheerfully instructed (or at least, that's what Sabine had translated for her from the original German script). *Let your awareness float outside yourself until you are able to hear it: the tickle of other people's thoughts.*

Libby scrunched up her face in concentration and tried it. She desperately wanted to hear the tickle of her parent's thoughts ….

But nothing.

Absolutely nothing. The only thing Libby could hear was the rattle of the station wagon's engine.

She just couldn't focus.

And it didn't help that she felt dizzy again; familiar waves of nausea rolled from somewhere behind her eyes, then down into her throat. It was worse today than normal. It was so bad, in fact, that she had completely forgotten her top hat when leaving the house that morning. Libby always wore her top hat on her birthday. Always. Even to school. She wondered if it was a bad omen that she'd forgotten it.

She swallowed hard, trying to fight the nausea off as the station wagon rumbled down Beach Boulevard, toward Biloxi. To her right, the Gulf waters rippled under the August sun, flat and grey. Like the sky. Like the mood in her chest.

Suddenly, the station wagon turned into a parking lot

Chapter 1

beside a marina. Her dad killed the engine. Beyond them, boats bobbed in the water between wooden pilings.

Without saying a word, her parents climbed out of the car, her mom carefully lifting the birthday cake she had been holding as she left the front passenger seat. She struggled a bit with the weight of it, even though Libby knew the cake wasn't *that* heavy.

In fact, Libby noticed that every day, her mom's energy faded a little. It wasn't just that white streak in her hair growing wider and wider against the black, it was everything about her ... like something was slowly leaking away. No amount of trips to the doctor could solve the mystery behind her illness, but Libby couldn't help but stay up at night and worry what would happen when that white streak took over altogether ....

She pushed the thought down and scrambled out of the car to help her mom, but Gretchen Frye just smiled and waved her off.

"Go on, Birthday Girl!" she said excitedly. "There's something for you down that dock!"

It was hard to see much of anything with all the people strolling between the boats. But then Libby noticed the shiny frame of Esmerelda waving excitedly at them from the end of a pier, shouting, "Hurry-up-Liberty-Frye!" followed by, "I-do-declare-you-there! Big-bellied-man-with-the-hamburger! And-you! Lady-with-too-much-makeup! Could-you-please-just-step-aside? Fryes-coming-through! Yes-you-there! Step-aside! Step-aside!"

That's how Esmerelda spoke to everyone. It annoyed Uncle Frank so much that sometimes he just shut her down completely. After all, no one—not even the genius who invents them—likes being insulted by a robot.

"Please-just-move-*out-of-the-way!*" Esmerelda continued, moving her little robot arms like a traffic cop.

"Those cognitive enhancements Uncle Frank installed are only making her *worse*," muttered Peter Frye, but Libby was already running down the pier toward the robot.

"Esmerelda!" she cried. "I didn't know you would be here!"

"And miss today?" came a gruff voice. Libby turned just as an old, lanky man with wiry brown and grey hair poked his head through the cabin door of a large sailboat. "And where's your special hat?" he added, eying her bare head.

"Uncle Frank!" exclaimed Libby in delight.

"Always got to hog the spotlight, don't you?" grunted another voice, and in the next moment, Salvador McCool huffed around the side of the cabin and stood, bowlegs and all, in the middle of the boat deck. Uncle Frank's old war buddy grinned at Libby with his three teeth, evidently forgetting he'd left his dentures somewhere. "Happy birthday, kid!"

It wasn't until then that Libby really put the clues together:

For starters, there was Uncle Frank, of course, who was currently moving out of the cabin with the help of his mobile unit, which now included bizarre, mechanical appendages that bent and straightened like spider legs. They made strange, clicking sounds against the polished, wooden boat deck.

Second, there was the boat itself. It looked like a refurbished pirate ship or something—a real fixer-upper—with weird, metal contraptions sticking off masts and out of windows, glinting in the sunlight.

One of them, Libby recognized, was a windmill made out of recycled scrap metal. Another was a solar panel composed of several long cells attached by hinges so the panel could bend to various surfaces. There were tons of other things, too—patched

Chapter 1

metal and riveted things—that she wouldn't be able to classify if her life depended upon it ... except for this one fact:

They were all the unmistakable handiwork of Uncle Frank.

And finally, if all of this was not enough to clue her in completely, on the side of the boat, in giant, cursive letters, she saw:

Liberté.

Libby blinked and looked again. The name was still there, floating in white script. She didn't know what was up with the strange spelling, but there was no mistaking the rest of it. For better or for worse, it was most definitely her name.

"We *told* you!" Her dad grinned as he swooped her into a bear hug. "Was this worth the wait or what, Sassafras?"

"It's been so hard for us not to spill the beans," her mom added excitedly. She leaned toward the guardrail and handed the birthday cake to Sal. "We'll join you all later; your dad and I are going to get some things for the picnic!"

Libby looked from one to the other, unsure of what she was more surprised by: Uncle Frank's refurbished yacht or the fact that Ginny had kept a secret for so long. So much for reading the tickle of other people's thoughts ....

"C'mon!" said Ginny, grabbing Libby's arm and tugging her toward to deck. "We're taking a tour around the bay first!"

Even though Libby knew how to put on a life vest, Ginny still insisted on reading the instructions pamphlet to her line by line. By the time she'd finished, they were already floating away from the pier.

Libby looked up and waved at her parents who were waving back, shouting things like "Don't get too close to the side, girls!" and "Uncle Frank, remember, be back in an hour! It's a bay cruise, not a voyage to Horn Island!"

Uncle Frank grunted in response and then barked instructions from the wheel, simultaneously pulling cranks and pushing buttons while steam hissed from pipes and sails groaned up the masts.

When they'd maneuvered out of the marina and into the bay, Libby managed to make her way to Uncle Frank's side as Ginny inspected some sort of clipboard, loudly inquiring about emergency flares and safety equipment, ticking things off as she ran through her list. Sal hopped around, hoisting here and pulling there until the sails ballooned with air and the ship lurched forward, as if tugged by an invisible hand.

And even though all of this was terribly exciting, Libby couldn't help but notice that the farther she drifted away from her mother, the dizzier and more nauseated she felt ….

"You ready for your *real* birthday surprise?" Uncle Frank grinned, glancing over at her from the wheel.

Libby tried to look intrigued, but she was having a hard time staying upright, much less carrying on a conversation. Besides, if she opened her mouth right now, she wasn't entirely sure what might come out. So she kept her lips clamped together and nodded in reply.

"Then follow me, m'lady," he said with a wink, turning toward the cabin. "Esmerelda, come take the wheel, would you? Remember, just like we've practiced!"

Libby staggered down the stairs after Uncle Frank, grateful for the railings to hold on to as the boat swayed from side to side. Her pupils dilated from the cabin's sudden dimness as she blinked about for any sign of a bathroom, just in case. She heard the click-click-clicking of Uncle Frank's bizarre mobile unit appendages as he moved toward a metal contraption that hovered in the shadows.

Chapter 1

When her eyes adjusted, Libby could see that the contraption looked like a cross between a pot-bellied stove and one of those old-fashioned submarine periscopes she'd seen before in movies. Uncle Frank was already beside it, twisting dials, adjusting this and moving that as the machine whined and whirred.

Libby moved closer to the strange machine, almost feeling drawn to it by an invisible force. Now, she could see that on the other side, a rubber ducky inner tube lined with netting sat on a square plate of thick, dark glass. The netting of the inner tube cradled a small, lopsided box wrapped in birthday paper.

"What *is* that?"

"Well, that's your birthday present, of course!"

Libby shook her head, momentarily forgetting all about her dizziness and nausea. "No, I mean this machine thing."

"Ah!" Uncle Frank paused mid-dial and beamed back at her. "What you are seeing is the crowning achievement of my lifetime, Libby! I've been working on this since the 1970s, after I realized that a peculiar chap whom I encountered during my Flying Tiger days might not have been as daft as I'd suspected. But that is another story altogether—actually, one that ties into those moonstone necklaces I gave to you and Ginny last year. In any case, there is a very good reason why I have this contraption on board as we set sail this fine morning! Now, how do you feel about teleportation?"

"Tele …." Libby paused, struggling to keep up with her eccentric great uncle. "But we're supposed to be back in an hour!"

"And so we shall!" he exclaimed, his voice booming with so much enthusiasm that Libby actually jumped a little. "But while we ply these familiar seas, your gift, my girl, will take another tour altogether. The teleportation of photons—nay, quantum entanglement itself—is mere child's play compared to what you are about to witness! And you, my dear grandniece, will be the first human being to ever lay eyes on such a demonstration.

"To wit, in mere moments, that superbly packaged cube of matter shall undergo a journey never before taken in the history of recorded science. And at journey's end, we shall find it floating on the other side of the bay, just waiting for you to scoop it up! Imagine the crew's confusion when we bring it aboard!"

Libby blinked, turning from her Uncle Frank to the birthday parcel cheerily sitting inside the rubber ducky inner tube.

"Here's to birthdays, Liberty Frye!" cried Uncle Frank, just as a bolt of lightning flashed through the open cabin door above, briefly illuminating the room. A clap of thunder rattled in the near distance. "And put on this helmet, just in case. Ready?"

"Well I …." Libby stopped, her voice drowning into the whines of the machine as everything around them instantly went pitch black. She wasn't sure if it was the problem with her head or something else, but it felt as if the cabin was suddenly swirling around her, faster and faster. Cracking sounds of thunder shivered in the air as Libby stumbled in the darkness, searching for Uncle Frank.

"What's happening?" she cried, looking around the room, but there was nothing to be seen but the electric swirl of darkness. And then, from somewhere in the chaos, she heard Uncle Frank yelling:

"Hold on to your helmet, Libby! And don't touch anything else, whatever you do!"

"I *didn't* touch anything!" Libby yelled back, but in the next moment, a shudder more forceful than the others combined shook her off her feet, and before Libby could stop herself, she felt the cold, hard press of metal slam against her skin.

Chapter 2

The Terrible Darkness

When Libby opened her eyes, a single light bulb glowed from the cabin ceiling.

"Steady, kiddo. You took quite a spill back there."

She groaned, instantly aware of the ache in her temples. She reached up to her forehead. Uncle Frank had put a cool cloth there, but underneath, her fingers felt the rise of a bump, just above her left brow. And she was lying on one of the bunk beds, she suddenly realized.

"How long have I been … out?" she asked, confused by everything around her.

"Not long. I …." Uncle Frank paused and turned his face so that she could no longer see his expression. When he spoke next, his words sounded choked, as if he was trying not to cry:

"I'm so sorry, Libby. That was extremely irresponsible of

me. I let my enthusiasm get in the way and I ... I'd never forgive myself if something had happened ...." He stopped and swallowed, still looking away. Then he shook his shaggy, brown-and-silver head, burying his face in his hands.

"Hey, I'm alright, Uncle Frank," said Libby, trying to sound perkier than she felt, because her head was killing her. "Did it work at least?"

Uncle Frank made a funny snorting noise. His voice was somber when he replied, "In a way, Libby. I suppose you could say that it did."

Libby frowned, trying to understand where Uncle Frank's moodiness was coming from. Normally, he grew positively ecstatic over his inventions, especially when demonstrating them for the first time. And this—his self-proclaimed life's work—was a pretty huge deal. Astronomical, in fact. Libby knew nothing of teleportation except silly stuff in books and movies, but she knew enough to realize that what Uncle Frank had just achieved could change the world ... if he actually shared it.

"Well, that's awesome!" she exclaimed, but then she let her head fall back against the pillow. "Do you happen to have an aspirin or anything?"

Uncle Frank turned and whirred over to a cabinet. A minute later, he returned with a bottle of water and two small, orange pills.

"Here you go, kiddo," he mumbled distractedly.

Libby watched Uncle Frank's face as she chewed the baby aspirin. It dawned on her that he seemed just as confused as she was, but in a different way, she guessed. He kept staring over at the contraption, a stunned look on his face, like a mixture between awe and fear. Disbelief, too. His eyes shifted back to Libby.

Chapter 2

"How do you feel?" he asked, watching her closely.

"Okay," she lied, pushing herself upright.

Only then, from a sitting position, could she see Uncle Frank's contraption across the room. Half of it lay on its side, pipes and pieces and glass scattered about the floor, while the periscope-looking portion of the thing was bent in the middle, like a giant dog had chewed on it.

"I ... did all of *that?*" she asked, incredulous, suddenly forgetting all about her aches and pains. "Oh, Uncle Frank, I'm so sorry! I—"

Uncle Frank silenced her with a wave of his hand.

"Relax, kiddo, you couldn't have possibly done all that. That pipe is thicker than you are—I've no idea how it bent in two like that. I'm just glad you're alright."

"But your invention," she gulped. "How are you ever going to ...?" She stopped, her gaze locking on the other side of the mangled periscope. She blinked and looked again. Then, slowly, she turned back to Uncle Frank. "I thought you said ... you said it *worked.*"

"I said sort of."

"But the rubber ducky—and the present—they're still here!"

Uncle Frank nodded, and his voice had grit in it when he said, "I think it's time for us to join the others, Libby."

When Libby reached the staircase and glanced up through the open cabin door, the sky outside was pitch black.

"Uncle Frank ... um, has there been some weird eclipse or something?" she asked nervously as she climbed the stairs. "There was nothing about an eclipse on the weather channel, was there?"

"Eclipse ...," Uncle Frank repeated, as if thinking the idea over, but then he said nothing more.

Libby bit her lower lip. She stepped onto the deck and peered through the darkness, just as the shiny glint of Esmerelda caught her eye. Perhaps it was the stillness of the little robot that seemed peculiar. She sat near the bow, surrounded by Ginny and Buttercup, their eyes looming eerily in the gloom.

On the starboard side of the boat, Libby could see Sal standing by the guardrail, gazing into the sky. Otherwise, the *Liberté* was still and silent, as if all sound had been sucked from the sea.

"What's going on?" she practically whispered, but in the stillness, her voice came out like a fog horn.

She glanced at Ginny, hoping for some piece of information, but Ginny's giant, brown eyes just blinked back. Sal turned around, however, and Libby noticed that he held something in his hands that looked like an elaborate metal semi-circle attached to a microscope lens.

"No use, Frye," he muttered, glancing at Uncle Frank. "Not a reference point to be found for this thing—no sun, no stars, no horizon, nothin'."

The clicking of Uncle Frank's mobile unit legs stopped beside Libby. She turned to look at her great uncle, then back at Sal. "What ... are you trying to find?"

For a moment, no one responded.

"Our location," Ginny finally replied in a trembling voice. "We're trying to find our *location* with a *bleeping antique sextant!*"

At this bit of information, Libby's arms prickled into bumps, and she had the sudden sensation that she had awakened to a bizarre nightmare—the kind where you know you are still sleeping, but you can't shake yourself out of it, so you just have to go along with things until you wake up. She swallowed,

Chapter 2

ignoring the jab in her forehead, and took a deep breath, forcing herself to concentrate.

"Uncle Frank," she said as quietly as she could—mostly because Ginny looked like she'd freak out if someone so much as sneezed, "could you please tell me why Sal is looking for our location?"

"Because nothing else works!" snapped Ginny, jumping to her feet, her hands balled into fists at her sides. "The radio is dead, and no one's phone has a signal! It's like we're stuck in the middle of an apocalypse! What if I have hypothermia? Or dehydrate out here? What if no one sees us until ... until this horrible thing has blown over? And what *is* this thing *anyway?*" she continued, now waving her arms about, becoming more and more frantic with each syllable. "What if ...?"

"Calm down, kid," barked Sal McCool. "You're the girl who flew across the world in my P-40, remember? And, according to everything I've heard from you on at least a hundred different occasions, the *same* girl who jumped into a freezing river ... *and* followed Libby into a creepy cave to save her parents, right? If you can do all that, surely you can handle this!"

"But *this* isn't a cave!" Ginny screamed back, pointing to the water. "Do you know the worst thing that's in a cave during winter? Bears!" she shouted before anyone could reply. "And they're hibernating! So, no, I won't *just calm down* because you know what's down *here?*"

Libby wrinkled her nose. "Fish?" she suggested.

"Sharks!" snapped Ginny, who was now officially hysterical. "And *eels!* And, and ... octopi! I HATE octopi! They're like, smart!"

"Ginny, take a breath," Uncle Frank said, his voice stern and calm. "No octopus will get you in the Biloxi Bay, I am quite certain. And you will not dehydrate as I have lots and lots of water—in fact, I have a distiller that makes its own from the sea. And as far as hypothermia, you are on a dry deck with dry clothes and a warm cabin should you need it."

Ginny hiccupped, but otherwise, it looked like Uncle Frank had made some progress.

"That's better," he added gently, and then glanced over at Sal. "The thing to be concerned about isn't our location; it's what happened to our sun. *That's* what I can't make sense of."

"What about the other boats in the bay?" whimpered Ginny. "There were at least three!"

Uncle Frank shook his head. "I don't know. Maybe their equipment failed, too. Maybe it's simply too dark to see them."

"My-infrared-vision-has-already-determined-no-other-vessels-are-near," observed Esmerelda. "But-I-would-like-to-inform-Liberty-Fyre-that-her-heat-signature-is-a-peculiar-one-indeed-I—"

"But in regards to our *location*," cut in Uncle Frank, glaring at Esmerelda, "I can reasonably hypothesize that we are merely two or three miles from where we started. So all we need to do is keep calm and find our way back."

At this pronouncement, Sal lowered the sextant and looked at Uncle Frank long and hard. Even in the darkness, Libby could see Sal's expression: his mouth all twisted up like he'd just swallowed a bucket of seawater.

Then he said, "The minute you went below deck, Frank Frye, the wind died. Ergo, there's no way we've already traveled two or three miles from where we started unless we got picked up in a tornado like Dorothy! And I don't know about you, but I ain't no Dorothy! So mind telling me how you can *reasonably hypothesize* such a thing? Because we *should* be right smack-dab outside the marina!"

Chapter 2

Libby realized she'd been holding her breath. She exhaled, trying to calm the flutter in her heart. Everyone was acting so strangely, and she knew that if she didn't do something to diffuse the tension, Uncle Frank and Sal would get in another one of their squabbles, which was the last thing anyone needed at the moment.

"Well, when we were in the cabin," she offered before Uncle Frank had a chance to reply, "it sounded like a thunderstorm hit and then it got really dark all of the sudden." She looked at the faces floating before her. "So … what happened up here? What did *you* guys see?"

"We-did-see-a-bolt-of-lightning…," Esmerelda agreed.

"Yeah, and then everything got dark, too, and like, *weird*," Ginny added anxiously, her eyes darting around the deck. "I mean, we couldn't see much because of the sudden darkness, and it all happened so fast, but it was like …." She stopped, shaking her head as she glared at the deck floor.

"What, Ginny?" asked Uncle Frank, his voice strangely calm. Eager, even. "What was it like?"

"It was like that darned painting, that's what!" snapped Sal, turning to face them all. "You know, the squiggly one—the one that's always copied—*The Yell* or something?"

Then he pantomimed holding the sides of his face, his mouth open, eyes wide. Under any other circumstance, this would have been highly entertaining, but Libby was too caught up in the mystery to appreciate Sal's ridiculous appearance.

"Ah-yes-The-Scream. A-series-of-four-paintings-by-the-Norwegian-artist-Edvard-Munch-created-between-1893-and-1910," noted Esmerelda cheerfully. "It-is-one-of-the-most-copied-pieces-of-modern-times."

"Yeah! *The Scream*—I know the one you're talking about!"

agreed Ginny. "It's on someone's notebook at school. It's like the whole sky and the world around is twisting and melting at the same time, and there's this person in the front, facing you, twisting with the rest of it! It *was* like that, come to think of it. All stretchy and stuff—only darker; if it hadn't been for the lightning bolts, I wouldn't have seen anything!"

"So you saw it, too?" Sal asked, obvious relief in his voice. "Kid, I thought maybe I was going crazy!"

Libby watched Uncle Frank as they all spoke. He had been quiet this whole time, but it wasn't just like he was listening. It was like he was *figuring out* something.

"Does this make any sense to you?" she asked, turning to him. "You're the only one who hasn't said anything, Uncle Frank, and you haven't explained why that rubber ducky is still here, either."

"Yeah, and what's with the contraption that I helped you haul on board?" Sal added. "I suspect *that's* got something to do with our plight if I know you, Frye. So out with it, man! What have you gotten us into?"

But Uncle Frank just sat there, lips clamped together and eyebrows knitted so close that it looked like he'd sprouted a caterpillar.

"Uncle Frank, are you going to tell them or not?" asked Libby. "'Cause if you won't, then I will. They deserve to know."

"Know what?" demanded Ginny.

Libby sighed and stared at Uncle Frank, giving him one last chance, but he just shrugged and scowled harder.

"Well it's …." She paused, unsure how to say it exactly.

"WHAT?" shouted Ginny and Sal together.

"Uncle Frank's made a teleportation device," she blurted,

and then she stared at the deck below her feet, not wanting to meet her great uncle's glare.

"A *teleportation device*," snorted Sal. "That's impossible, kid, even for your *genius* Uncle Frank. You think that's what this is all about? A *teleportation device?*" And before anyone could answer, he dissolved into guffaws of laughter.

"And that," said Uncle Frank, "is why I didn't want to tell them."

"I can die a happy man now—I've seen and heard it all!" gasped Sal between chortles.

"It's true!" said Libby, feeling her temper rise. For just a second, a flicker of light danced somewhere in the horizonless sky before disappearing once more into the black. But it was weird. Just as the flicker came and went, so did that strange feeling in her head ....

"That's why we were on the boat today," she continued, forcing herself to concentrate. "Uncle Frank had a present for me ...."

"A rubber ducky?" suggested Sal, still choking with laughter.

"No! My present was *in* the rubber ducky!" said Libby, growing increasingly agitated. "And Uncle Frank was going to teleport it somewhere in the bay, where we would pick it up. That's when—"

"Hoo-hoo-hoo!" wheezed Sal, dabbing at his eyes. "This is getting better and better!"

"Well-I-have-seen-it-too," said Esmerelda. "I-believe-Liberty-Frye-is-telling-the-truth."

"I've no doubt Liberty Frye is telling the truth," Sal said, sobering somewhat. "It's that nut-head uncle of hers that I'm speculatin' on! Seriously, Frank. I know you're long in the tooth and all, but this is just plain delusional. There is no such thing as true teleportation! It's been proven. Certainly not of a rubber ducky birthday present!"

"As Libby has already stated," Uncle Frank explained, glaring at Sal, "it wasn't the rubber ducky that was intended as her present. As a matter of fact, I might as well tell you that it was *your* gift for her that I'd placed *in* the rubber ducky!"

Sal McCool took a sharp breath as his eyes narrowed. "The *point I'm making,*" he resumed in a brittle voice, "is that this is where I draw the line. Robots? Sure, it's weird but doable; invent them all you want and I'll give you credit. A steam-powered sail ship? Again, crazy, but it was done in the early 1900s, so why not now? Hence, doable. That mobile unit of yours? Downright creepy but—"

"Doable," said Ginny.

Sal nodded. "But a teleportation device is not just *not*-doable, it doesn't exist!"

"Which is why I invented one!"

Sal raised his hands in the air and backed away a few steps.

"Fine. You invented it? When, exactly, during the eight months I've had the displeasure of your company, have you even worked on it? Riddle me that!"

Libby couldn't be sure—it was far too dark to see clearly—but it looked like Uncle Frank's face had just turned the shade of a grape lollypop.

"I've been working on it for *decades,* McCool," Uncle Frank growled. "If you'd ever troubled yourself to visit my study, that fact would be readily apparent!" Clicking over to the bow, he stretched his arms out, gripping the railings at both sides of the bow as he looked out to sea.

Sal rolled his eyes. "I'm no genius, but I happen to know teleportation cannot occur to complex matter, thank you very much! So how do you expect me to believe that *you've* developed a way to teleport a rubber ducky?"

"Well, that's just the thing," said Uncle Frank without turning. "I didn't."

At this, everyone whipped around to look at him. Uncle Frank remained at the bow, facing the sea.

"I didn't teleport the rubber ducky," he resumed quietly, the sound of his voice carrying oddly in the still, black air. "I think I teleported the *boat!*"

Chapter 3

Flying Fish

Libby had never heard so much silence come from Salvador McCool's general direction.

It was Ginny who finally spoke up.

"Are you telling us," she half-whispered, half-shrieked, "that *we've* been teleported?"

"I believe so," said Uncle Frank, sounding almost as incredulous as she did. "It was supposed to be the rubber ducky, but then that storm came on and something must have hijacked my machine …."

"So, you can't even beam us back?" Sal blurted, his tone mildly panicked.

"Relax, McCool. Like I said, we're only a mile or two out from where we started. I imagine we're sitting where the rubber ducky was *supposed* to be floating at this moment."

Chapter 3

"But the sky …," began Ginny, and Uncle Frank nodded.

"I know. It should be simple to turn back to shore, but whatever caused this," he waved his hand into the darkness around them, "must have knocked out the whole grid. There's not a single light from the shore—not a light anywhere. At least we have generators on board; it's just our communications that seemed to have malfunctioned."

"Flares!" said Ginny, her voice growing desperate. "We can use the emergency flares!"

"For what, Ginny? Whatever has happened to our power has happened to everyone else's. No boat's going to venture out right now; I'm afraid we'll have to sit tight until the radio or the daylight returns, whichever comes first—I'm not too particular."

Sal glowered, flicking a rope with his fingers. "Well, that's very open-minded of you!"

Uncle Frank didn't respond to that. He just kept staring out into the pitch black, as if waiting for something to answer.

The sun, probably.

Libby turned from him to Sal, then to Ginny and Esmerelda, where they sat huddled together, big, brown eyes next to glassy grey, both pairs equally wide with alarm. It was a bad omen, thought Libby, when even a robot looked scared.

As if sensing her thoughts, Buttercup waddled up to her and nuzzled his head against her leg. Libby scooped him up in her arms and buried her face in his feathers. The thought of being teleported was confusing enough, but the realization that her parents were somewhere out there, standing in the dark and panicking over what had happened, made her heart ache. They'd already been through so much in the past year, all because of her, and now, she couldn't help but wonder if her freaky powers had somehow brought this on, too; just like all the other weird things that inevitably happened whenever she was around.

When Libby was younger, she'd always thought these *things* were coincidences: lights turning on and off on their own, objects—and sometimes, even people—appearing just when Libby thought hard about them, all kinds of bizarre things that she'd always assumed were coincidences … until eight months ago. That's when Libby and her parents had gone to Germany for Christmas and everything Libby knew about herself—about life—had changed.

Because that's when her parents were poisoned and Libby kidnapped by a witch named Zelna. When Libby managed to escape and find help from a horrifically ugly witch in the woods named Sabine (only Sabine was a good witch—apparently, there are a surprising number of undercover witches in the world), she finally discovered the truth: that Zelna was actually Libby's great aunt!

But it got even worse, because Libby learned she was herself descended from this same line of witches called the Coven of Hessen, as was her mother, and that enormous power, more than those before her combined, flowed through Libby's veins.

Thankfully, between Ginny flying across the ocean and finding them, Uncle Frank's magical moonstone amulets and a potion that Sabine made to revive Libby's parents, they'd all escaped Zelna's clutches relatively unharmed. Except for whatever caused the growing white streak in Gretchen Frye's hair, of course ….

But Libby knew her mother's mysterious health problem wasn't the only souvenir they'd brought back. The other was something that grew stronger with each day, a force inside of Libby that sent waves of nausea from behind her eyes, then

Chapter 3

through her forehead. Whenever this happened, other strange things happened, too. The knowledge of this terrified her—mostly because she didn't know what it meant. Or how to control it. Or why it was happening more and more ….

"Well, I don't know about the rest of you," Uncle Frank finally said, "but I could use a good, strong cup of coffee. What do you say we wait this out in the cabin? I'll show you all how to use the generator—it's pretty ingenious, if I do say so myself."

And with that, he click-clicked across the deck and made his way down the stairs. Ginny got up and walked after him, followed by Esmerelda and then even Sal. No one said a word.

Libby hugged Buttercup tighter and took another look at the black, vast sky. Then she squeezed back the panic in her chest, took a deep breath and headed for the stairs, too.

Below deck, she walked straight to one of the cabin bunks, feigning sleepiness as Uncle Frank and the others clanged about in the galley.

From where Libby lay, she could hear Uncle Frank explaining how his cabin generator ran off alternate power sources of solar, wind and even some kind of hydroelectric system he'd rigged up in the bilge. But it wasn't his voice that kept her awake, it was the rolling in her head that matched the panic in her chest. And while the baby aspirin had dulled the ache somewhat, those sickening waves in her head just wouldn't go away.

She wondered if her increased nausea had anything to do with her birthday; hadn't Sabine mentioned something about that before? Some nonsense about her own binary star system and cycles and the visibility of her power or something? Libby didn't know what any of it meant exactly, but she wished more than ever that she could talk to her mom about it.

The thought dragged a sob up Libby's throat. She swallowed

it down and shoved her face into the pillow. She'd give almost anything to go back to her birthday a year ago, before she knew of this power in her veins that did horrible things to the people she loved.

When sleep finally came, Libby dreamt wild, electric dreams of her parents awakening from the spell while in that horrid cave, pale and still as death; of Zelna's beautiful, cruel face as Libby lay on the stone table, watching as it seemed that her self and that of Zelna's began blending in the dark magic of the solstice; of the moonstone amulets exploding in the air with blue light, throwing Zelna away from Libby and dissolving the witch into particles of dazzling light that shrieked through the sky; of Ginny's huge eyes and of her own mother yelling words Libby could not understand before she fell, unconscious, to the floor. It all blurred together with flashes behind her eyes.

When she awoke, Libby just lay there for a moment in a cold sweat, panting, disoriented by her surroundings. Outside, she heard the faint honking of Buttercup and inside, a steady rumble that could only be Sal's snores reminded her where she was.

Libby slipped from her bunk, careful not to awaken Ginny, whose right arm dangled from the bunk above, and tip-toed to the stairs leading up to the deck. She passed Sal on the way; he was splayed over a small, upholstered couch, mouth open, fast asleep. From here, she could see into the galley, where Esmerelda sat in the dining booth, upright and rigid, eyes closed as she recharged. Libby could just make out the cord plugged into a generator on the floor.

Libby edged around the couch and up the stairs, now pushing open the cabin door. It made low, creaky sounds in protest,

Chapter 3

just before a blast of light hit her square in the face, blinding her for a good three seconds. When she'd adjusted to the light, she climbed up on deck and closed the door behind her, then looked around in amazement.

The sky above was dazzling, so blue it looked fake—and the air was cool and fresh, like an early spring morning. All around, deep aquamarine water stretched as far as she could see, except for one tiny spot of greenery—floating like one of her mother's famous St. Paddy's day cupcakes—on the horizon.

She was still staring at the land when she noticed Uncle Frank sitting in his mobile unit by the mainmast.

"Where are we?" she called, walking toward him.

Uncle Frank jerked his head, as if she'd startled him from a reverie. Then she saw Sal's sextant resting on his lap and several navigational charts stuffed into one of the side pockets of his mobile unit, but he hadn't been using them or the sextant when she'd come on deck. Uncle Frank glanced at Libby, his eyes wide with wonder.

"Just … wait a moment," he whispered, lifting a shaking finger to the water. Libby followed his gesture, seeing nothing but the deep, velvet ocean. But then, seconds later, a spot just below the surface turned jewel blue—like the water from a hotel swimming pool—and then ….

"Whoa!" Libby gasped, stumbling backward, and had it not been for the mast behind her, she would have fallen flat on her butt. She stood there, back pressed against the pole, as a huge, black whale with a swath of white belly rolled from the deep.

A sound like a low, moaning whistle filled the air before a swooshing noise displaced it and then, before Libby could think to close her mouth, the whale flipped a fin and swiveled upright with a foamy spray of water.

She squeezed her eyes shut, then opened them again. It was still there: a black, knobby behemoth so huge it almost looked like a submarine or something, except that its movements were graceful and smooth, like an acrobat in the water. And then she noticed for the first time a smaller shape keeping pace alongside it.

"Are those …?"

"Humpback whales," whispered Uncle Frank in amazement. "A cow and her calf, more specifically. We must be in their breeding grounds."

Before Libby could comment upon that improbability, he added, "Is Ginny awake yet?"

"N-no," stammered Libby.

"Good," said Uncle Frank, his eyes glued to the whales' movements. "Let's keep it that way until we can sort out how we're going to handle this."

Another spray of water shot into the air, dissolving into mist. Then, just as quickly as the whales had appeared, they rolled into the water once more, disappearing into the deep.

Libby stared at the place where the water rippled before smoothing over like silk. It wasn't until then that Uncle Frank's words sank in.

"… handle what?"

Uncle Frank cleared his throat and swiveled around to face her. The mechanical whir of his mobile unit sounded strange after those melodic, whistling moans from the sea.

"I've been on deck since all of you fell asleep," he replied. "I watched the sun rise over there," he pointed to the horizon in the east. "That was thirty minutes ago. You've been asleep for a little over an hour."

Libby swallowed, looking from the horizon to the golden

Chapter 3

glow above. She'd never seen the sun look so *clear* before, especially during the summer. The thought swam abstractedly in her head.

"Think about it, Libby. We set sail a little after ten in the morning; we haven't even been on the boat for three hours yet. What does that tell you?"

She stared down at her feet, trying to push the muddle out of her mind.

"I don't …." She paused, forcing herself to break the facts down into digestible pieces. "Are you sure you didn't fall asleep, too, Uncle Frank?" she asked, looking up again to catch his expression. "Because otherwise, what you're saying is impossible. If you actually saw the sun *rise*, that means we just slept through an entire day. But you're saying we've only been out for three hours, so it should only be around one in the afternoon!"

"Unless you consider another possibility."

"What?" she asked, but part of her wondered if she even wanted to know. She crossed her arms in front of her, as if bracing for his reply.

"Libby, what do you know about humpback whales?"

"Not much," she admitted as an ominous feeling crept inside.

"And what do you know about those?" Uncle Frank continued, pointing down the deck a ways.

Again following her great uncle's gesture, Libby now saw several narrow glints of silver lying near the bow. She walked toward them, her heart thumping in an odd sort of way.

"They're … fish," she said as soon as she was close enough to see.

"Flying fish," corrected Uncle Frank. "But you missed something."

Libby turned again just as a light breeze fluttered the loose jib, sending the rigging clanging against the mast. Behind the jib's canvas, she saw Buttercup shifting on his feet, jutting his neck out and then back again, as if in some kind of dance. She moved closer, only then noticing that he was not alone. A huge, white bird with a thick, hooked beak stood to the other side, pecking a fish.

For a moment, the bird paused and squawked at Buttercup—as if fearing the goose might eat its meal—and in reply, Buttercup squawked back, attempting the same, strange high-pitched sound.

Libby laughed. She'd never heard Buttercup imitate another bird before.

"What you're looking at is an albatross," Uncle Frank said, pushing a button on his mobile unit so the wheels folded up and the creepy spider legs jutted out in its place. "That may seem like a boring observation on marine life to you, but in actuality, all of these creatures are *clues*. Clues that, when combined with the sunrise, provide an irrefutable fact."

"Alright," said Libby, playing along. "What is this mysterious, *irrefutable* fact?"

She heard the clicking of Uncle Frank behind her and turned just as he came to a stop by her side. He took her hand into his, his warm, dark eyes as solemn as the sea.

"What I'm about to tell you will be upsetting, Libby. But I need your help. The most important thing is to keep our wits about us, alright? So, what do you want to hear first? The good or the bad?"

"Um ... the good?"

"Excellent choice." Uncle Frank pointed at the patch of green floating on the horizon. "Because the good news is, we're headed there. Once we land, we'll find a way to contact your

Chapter 3

parents first thing, okay? Our communications on board are still disabled for some reason, but I'm sure something over there will work."

"You've got a strange definition of good news," said Libby, frowning at the faraway land. "So what's the bad?"

Uncle Frank took a deep breath, which only added to Libby's unease. She'd never seen him so nervous before. Agitated, yes. Irritated, often. But nervous? That just wasn't his style. He let go of her hand, then rubbed the two of his together.

"Let me break it to you this way." He glanced at the albatross, then at the sea, then back to Libby. "Those whales we saw? They definitely do not exist in the Biloxi Bay. They don't exist in the entire Mississippi Sound, either ... not even in the entire Gulf of Mexico."

Libby felt tingles go up her back as her chest thrummed uneasily. Her stomach suddenly felt like it was being squeezed inside a giant's fist.

"And this albatross," he continued, "it doesn't travel over the North Atlantic. Nor does that species of flying fish. Do you understand what I'm trying to tell you, Libby?"

Libby swallowed hard. The pounding in her chest pounded harder. "That ... that we're not in the Biloxi Bay anymore?"

"We're not even close to the Biloxi Bay," he answered, his voice laced with disbelief. "Because we've actually teleported quite a distance from where I had calculated. So far, in fact, that we're several *time zones* away. To be more precise, Libby—and this is where I really need you to keep your wits about you ...."

"*What?*" Libby practically shouted.

"Well," Uncle Frank said, his voice squeezed into a hoarse whisper, "I'm fairly certain we're somewhere in the South Pacific!"

Chapter 4

The Atoll Island

"You're *FAIRLY CERTAIN?*"

"Correct," said Uncle Frank, blinking back at her. "My track record for identifying our location hasn't been great, admittedly, but based upon—"

"*In the SOUTH PACIFIC,*" she choked out, and she couldn't believe what she was saying, even as she said it. "Like, *Hawaii*, or something?"

"That's in the North Pacific, Libby. I'd say we're further south ... and ... out."

"*Out?*"

"That is to say ... er, it gets a bit tricky due to the International Dateline, so it depends upon your perspective, of course. Technically, we could be east, but in terms of what you might imagine, I'd say west ...."

Chapter 4

"What?"

"Well, it's the dateline, you see," continued Uncle Frank, growing enthusiastic. He reached into the pocket of his mobile unit and pulled out a navigational chart, now straightening it between his hands as the breeze tugged it this way and that. "Fascinating how it works, really. It cuts right down the Pacific and ...."

"I don't care about the *dateline* right now, Uncle Frank! Just tell me where we *are!*"

Uncle Frank lowered the chart to his lap.

"Well, I'm guessing we're closer to the Kingdom of Tonga or the Cook Islands. Or perhaps it could be Bora Bora, I'm really quite at a loss."

"You're telling me," said Libby, trying very hard not to hyperventilate, "that we're somewhere in the *Pacific Ocean*."

"Hmm, yes."

"Like, far, far away in the Pacific, not Honolulu away."

"Indeed."

"Just floating out here in the South Seas ...."

"That's a rather bleak perspective, but—"

"And other than that, you don't know *where* we are ...."

"Well, hold on, Libby. I do know—"

"And you want me to *keep my wits* about me?"

Uncle Frank frowned, folded up the chart and then placed it back into the side pocket.

"Clearly, you're upset," he said, turning to her. "But it isn't as bad as it sounds. Sal's a whiz with the sextant, and once he's up, I'm sure we'll have a better grasp on our location. I myself was relying on the GPS for nautical direction, but unfortunately, it seems anything dependent upon satellites is kaput out here. Besides, we'll reach land soon and we'll know our location with certainty then. Think of it as an adventure, Libby!"

"An *adventure* …."

Uncle Frank nodded.

Libby took a deep breath, but it felt like her chest would crack from the panic swelling inside.

"An *adventure* is something you *choose* to do, Uncle Frank!"

"I disagree, Libby. Most adventures are unintentional, that's what makes them—"

"*This* is a *catastrophe!*" she cut him off, waving her arms about her. "We're lost in the middle of the South Pacific on an antique sailboat with a robot, a goose and … and an *albatross*, Uncle Frank! Do you have any *idea* how scared my parents must be right now?"

"Kiddo, I'm sorry," he said, his eyes warm with feeling. "I'm not trying to make light of this, but what am I supposed to do? We've got to stay calm and … and optimistic."

"Optimistic? My mom is out there somewhere freaking out. She's really, *really* sick, Uncle Frank! The last thing she needs is the stress of seeing us vanish into thin air! Did you think about that?"

"Well, no. And I agree it's not ideal."

Libby didn't know why, but something about the way he said that made her so upset she felt like her head might explode. Her eyes popped with tears, her nails digging into balled fists.

"This is *way* past *not ideal!* Did it ever occur to you that teleporting *anything* around human beings might not be such a great idea? You didn't even *warn* us! You get so caught up in all your crazy inventions that you don't even care about …."

She stopped, so agitated that she couldn't even finish, and the spinning in her head felt so out of control that she was half

Chapter 4

afraid something else horrible would happen if she didn't calm down. So she turned, only to see Ginny climb onto the deck followed by Sal. Libby ran toward them, her face burning hot, her eyes brimming with tears.

"Sorry, 'scuse me," she blurted, pushing past them to go down the stairs, slamming the door behind her. Below deck, she flung herself onto her bunk, trying to calm down, but the mental image of her parents staring in horror as a giant sailboat disappeared from the Biloxi Bay made the pounding in her head and chest even worse.

And what about tomorrow, when the lady from Social Services would come to check on Ginny? What were her parents going to say?

Oh, yeah, that foster kid who's staying with us ... you can't visit her right now because she's, uh ... teleported?

Libby's parents would join the list of cruddy foster families Ginny had already been removed from, and it wouldn't even remotely be their fault!

And *that* thought made Libby even more upset because for the past eight months, Libby couldn't tell *anyone* how frustrating it was to share a room with someone who constantly corrected you while doing everything exactly right, and how lonely it was to feel like you'd lost your best friend and gained an annoying sister.

But that wasn't even the worst of it. Because, as if watching your mother slip away while enduring the incessant goody-goodiness of your best-friend-turned-nagging-sibling-roommate wasn't bad enough, she had this *head* thing that made her feel like she was going crazy. The only person who might understand was her mother, but since returning from Germany, her mom was completely uninterested in addressing anything related to their powers. Rather, she seemed scared of it. The only guidance Libby had was the little book Sabine had given her, and as far as *that* went, Libby had made little progress on anything more advanced that a few basic spells for things like removing toenail fungus or something ... but anyone could do that if they just followed the instructions.

In fact, the most Libby had been able to achieve with her actual *powers* was a brief, telepathic communication with her favorite tree in their front yard—the one that produced her magical, purple berries. She'd learned her tree's name was Bartulby, the son and only living heir of Barvultmir, and that he wasn't very happy about the situation in Eastern Europe. But before Libby could learn anything more about his feelings on the matter, her connection with him had been lost.

Since then, really awkward things happened whenever she tried to reestablish communication, like the time she'd somehow turned his leaves into baby-blue flowers (and she could tell that totally made him furious), but nothing actually useful ever came from her efforts.

All in all, in the past eight months, Libby had never felt so alone and confused in her life. And the feelings she'd kept bottled up for so long now squeezed out of her in gasps and sobs.

When Libby finally calmed down enough to notice, she realized she could hear everyone talking on the deck above her. No one sounded particularly upset. Usually it was Ginny who freaked out, but instead, Libby could hear her insisting Sal dab some sunscreen on that bald head of his, then informing Uncle Frank that, according to her *Guide to Healthcare on the Seas* (naturally, Ginny had brought this with her), they should all apply mosquito repellant ASAP because they did *not* want to get the

Chapter 4

dengue fever while in the South Pacific. Then the low groan of Uncle Frank's bizarre steam contraptions that helped raise and lower the sails drowned out the rest of Ginny's commentary.

Libby got up and wobbled toward the galley sink, where she splashed water over her face and dried off with a dish towel, hoping she looked somewhat presentable. She was embarrassed to face everyone after her outburst, but it was better to get it over with.

At least Esmeralda hadn't witnessed her meltdown; the little robot was still seated in the booth next to the generator, eyes closed. A little light at the base of her neck blinked green, so Libby unplugged the cord from her back and flipped the tiny switch. As Esmerelda's eyes fluttered open, Libby turned to go up the stairs to the deck above.

The wind whipped her long, light brown hair in a million directions as soon as she opened the cabin door. She grabbed as many loose strands as she could with one hand while using her other to steady herself. Her footing was still pretty awkward, but at least she wasn't as shaky as when they'd first set out.

On the deck, she could see the ocean had lost its silkiness. Its lazy, velvet ripples had turned into jagged peaks that sprayed against the hull. The air felt sharper, too, and the sails above tugged with the wind, forming arcs of white that pushed them forward with a speed she hadn't expected.

Ginny and Sal sat at the bow with Buttercup between them, backs to Libby, facing the sea, so that they blocked the island in the distance from Libby's view. The albatross must have taken off because it wasn't visible anywhere, and Uncle Frank sat by the wheel, his eyes fixed straight ahead.

Libby moved in short, jerky steps toward him, grabbing ropes and cables along the way to steady herself. She hoped they weren't tied to anything important. When she reached Uncle Frank, he arched a bushy brow at her.

"Better?"

"I'm sorry, Uncle Frank," she blurted, throwing her arms around his shoulders. "I didn't mean it, what I said earlier. Sometimes, I just feel like I'm going crazy or something."

He patted her arm while keeping one hand on the wheel.

"Don't worry about, kiddo. I know you're going through a hard time right now."

She straightened back up and looked at him.

"You do?"

"Well … yeah," he answered uncomfortably. "It's not exactly … er, a secret, you know."

Libby wrinkled her nose as she thought about that. She hadn't mentioned her little behind-the-eyes-nausea situation since first telling her parents about it while they were still in Germany. But then they'd returned home and her parents had been busy with gaining custody of Ginny, and then her mom's weird illness started getting worse, and with everything else going on, Libby didn't want to worry anyone, so she'd just kind of dealt with it. Or thought she had ….

"So, like, how did you know?" she finally asked. "I never said anything."

Uncle Frank shot her a glance before returning his gaze to the sea.

"Well, listen, kiddo. You know you can come to me about anything. Anything at all and I'm here for you. But this … well, I reckoned it was more of a … er … you know, mother-daughter thing."

"Because of our powers, you mean?"

Chapter 4

"Well, I've never heard it put that way before, but ... but, sure. In fact, I think that's a very healthy perspective, Libby."

"You do?"

"Absolutely." He shifted in his mobile unit. "I'm glad to see you've got such an optimistic approach to your ... er ... journey."

"My journey?" repeated Libby, now thoroughly confused.

"You know ...." He cleared his throat as he shifted some more. "To ... ah .... well, to womanhood."

"To *womanhood?!*"

"Well ... yes." He paused to clear his throat again. "It's perfectly natural to be so confused and upset, what with all those hormones flooding through you and all. Goodness knows I remember what your father was like at that age! Maybe he was a year or two older when it started for him, but I've heard females mature at a much earlier age, especially this recent generation ...."

"Geez, Uncle Frank!"

"I'm just saying, Libby, you hold onto that attitude. It *is* a power, in a way. You ... er ... becoming a woman is ... uh ...." He took another deep breath, just as Libby peeked up at him. *His* face was the color of tropical fruit punch and he was staring so fiercely at the water before him that it looked like he was trying to conjure a kraken from the deep.

"Well, yes, it's indeed a great power," he concluded quickly. "And I'm—I'm proud of you!"

Libby groaned and threw her hands to her face. As if that trip to the store a few weeks ago to shop for certain undergarments hadn't been bad enough, to be having another coming-of-age conversation with *anyone*, much less her Uncle Frank was, well ....

"I think I want to die," she whispered, dizzy from embarrassment.

Or maybe it was the boat. It felt like the water rose and fell more violently than before, like they were sailing over the backs of camels.

"Nonsense," harrumphed Uncle Frank, but he didn't sound any less uncomfortable than she felt. "I know you might feel that way sometimes—perfectly natural, like I said. Those hormones can really sock a person in the gut. But puberty is nothing to be ashamed of, Libby. It's …."

"Ach! Please just stop!" she wheezed, cringing at the word. *Puberty.* So gross. What sick, twisted person came *up* with that term, anyway? "I wasn't talking about … my *journey*, Uncle Frank! I was talking about …."

"Uncle Frank! Libby!" cried Ginny. "Come look!"

Libby lunged forward, so eager to escape Uncle Frank that she almost forgot all about her wobbly sea legs. She didn't care if she had to drag herself through albatross poop at this point; she'd do anything to get away from that conversation.

"What?" she panted, stopping by Ginny's side. The water continued to roll under them, causing the bow to rise and fall so that the island disappeared, then re-appeared from view.

"There!" Ginny said.

Libby looked again, just as the boat's bow dipped slightly so the distant, sandy shoreline came into view. From where they stood, she could see light, aquamarine water circling the island in multiple rings like a fancy, gemstone necklace. The further the rings looped from the land, the darker the blues and greens became.

"Yep," bellowed Sal from somewhere above them. "Looks like an atoll."

Libby glanced up, now seeing Sal perched on a rope ladder dangling from a mast far above, one leg bent on a rung with the

Chapter 4

other leg stretched to the one below, holding a telescope to his right eye. He looked like a featherless flamingo.

Libby squinted her eyes from the sun's glare. "What's an atoll?" she called up to him.

"A coral island surrounded by reefs—usually encircling a lagoon!" replied Sal, his voice laced with excitement.

Libby didn't see what was so great about an atoll that should rouse Sal's enthusiasm so much, but then he added, "I guess that explains the welcome party!"

It wasn't until then that Libby saw what Sal was so excited about:

"Canoes!" he cackled in delight. "Some resort must think we're a yacht they're expecting. They're sending canoes to escort us!"

Chapter 5

The Last Amulet

"It's just like the movies!" Ginny gushed, hopping excitedly up and down. "I wonder if they'll have flower leis and stuff!"

"I'd say they'll reach us in less than an hour," called Sal, climbing down the rope ladder. "We'll sail toward them and drop anchor just before the outer reef."

"Or ... one of those fire shows!" Ginny continued excitedly. "You know—the ones with drums and fire hoops and all that crazy dancing? You think they'll have that?"

Uncle Frank chuckled. "Well, if we're headed to shore, then there's one thing we oughta do before we start watching fire shows."

"What's that?" asked Libby.

Just then, Esmeralda appeared from the cabin with the birthday cake in her hands. The little robot frantically jerked

Chapter 5

this way and that, trying in vain to shield the flickering candles from the wind.

"We're celebrating your birthday, of course!" answered Uncle Frank. "We already missed it since we've, er, teleported a day ahead," he flicked a nervous gaze Libby's way, "so we might as well do this before we hit the resort. After all, your mother put a lot of trouble into this cake. She'd be insulted if we didn't enjoy it!"

"He's right," said Ginny, grabbing Libby's arm. "And besides, we're all starving."

Libby followed Ginny toward Uncle Frank's post by the wheel. Sal hobbled past them and disappeared through the cabin door, re-appearing moments later with a scowl and his hands behind his back. He grumpily joined in the *Happy Birthday* song that Esmerelda was already leading them in, which, in all honesty, sounded pretty terrible. Between a monotone robot and a couple of tone-deaf, geriatric World War II pilots, the only person who could carry a tune was Ginny.

When they'd finished, Esmerelda took the cake and headed back down the stairs to cut it up.

"I guess now is as good of a time as any," announced Sal, holding out the small, lopsided birthday gift he'd been hiding behind his back while throwing a dirty look Uncle Frank's way. "At least your genius uncle didn't manage to teleport *this*."

Libby took the mangled box that Sal had rescued from the rubber ducky, uncertain if she should be excited or a little scared.

"Open it!" said Ginny.

Most of the paper was already crushed about the edges, so Libby didn't bother being dainty; she ripped the wrapping apart and tipped the box over until a metallic, cloth satchel dropped from the mess.

For several seconds, Libby forgot to breathe. She just stared at the familiar-looking satchel in the palm of her hand. Uncle Frank seemed equally stunned; a low whistle escaped from his lips.

"Is this what I think it is?" she finally asked.

"If you mean the last moonstone amulet, then yup," said Sal. "'Course, it has absolutely no power since the other two were destroyed in that cave, but still, I thought you'd like it as a memento."

Uncle Frank looked shaken. "Wish you would have told me *that* was your gift, McCool. Things might have gone quite differently had I known …."

"And anyway," Sal continued, ignoring him, "since I've fulfilled my debt to *El Capitán* over here, getting rid of that thing ain't nothing but a pleasure!"

Libby opened the satchel and tipped it so the titanium chain slipped out, followed by the heavier *thunk* of the moonstone amulet. While this stone with its indigo blue color and wispy swirls of white exactly matched the moonstones she and Ginny had worn in Germany, instead of the familiar figure-eight shape, it was much larger and circular, and the center was carved out in the shape of four combined circles so the hollow middle looked almost like a four-leaf clover.

She stared at the amulet in her hand, a hundred memories rushing back to her from the last time she wore such a thing, and then her mind shifted to earlier this morning, when Uncle Frank had shown her his strange machine … and *this stone* had been in the rubber ducky.

A heavy, airless feeling crept over her.

Chapter 5

"Well, you like it or not?" demanded Sal.

"Oh!" Libby jerked her gaze from the amulet back to Sal. "I love it! Thank you!" she replied distractedly, slipping the chain over her head so the amulet hung around her neck. "It's just that, well, I was thinking about what you said earlier, Uncle Frank. When you said these necklaces are somehow related to that teleportation device of yours?"

"Wait!" commanded Ginny. "I'll be right back. I want to hear this!" Scrambling below deck, she reappeared seconds later with a package wrapped in newspaper. "But first," she continued, handing the package to Libby, "open this."

Libby looked the package over. There was something about it that seemed familiar, but she couldn't quite place what it was.

"Hurry up!" coaxed Ginny. "We need to get this birthday-thing finished before we reach that resort. 'Cause you know that once we're there, we're totally hitting the pool. I don't care that I didn't bring a swimsuit—they'll just have to let me swim in my jeans and t-shirt!"

Libby ripped apart the newspaper wrapping, the whole time grinning at the idea of Ginny dive-bombing a fancy resort pool, when she stopped at the sight of bright, balloon letters spread over the glossy cover of a comic book. The letters said:

AMAZING FANTASY
15
SPIDER
MAN

"It's just a reprint," said Ginny, shrugging sheepishly at Libby's confused expression. "A few years ago, one of my loser foster dads threw it in the trash, so I snagged it. I know comics aren't really your thing—you're always reading those boring books most people don't read until they're forced to in high school or something ...."

Libby had no idea about comics or reprints, so she said, "Cool—thanks, Ginny!" hoping it was the appropriate response.

"Do you even know what it's *about?*" demanded Ginny.

"Um, Spiderman?"

"Libby, you're holding the *first episode* of Spiderman *ever printed!*" exclaimed Uncle Frank. "This is the stuff of history, reprint or no!"

Ginny nodded once—a quick, very-pleased-with-herself nod. "Well, it's lucky those boys I tried to sell it to didn't think so, because if they had, you wouldn't have a present!"

Libby looked from the comic to Ginny, then to Uncle Frank. And from the way he was still staring at the thing, she wondered if Ginny ought to have given it to him instead.

"Remember the first day we met?" prompted Ginny, crossing her arms in front of her. "Remember, you were in that tree of yours with the purple berries?"

"Yeah," said Libby. "You told me I should be wearing a helmet."

"Well, safety should always be a priority," sniffed Ginny, smoothing a strand of hair that had worked loose from her ponytail. She tucked it into the rubber band, felt again, and when she was satisfied everything was back in place, she added: "Remember what I was *holding?*"

Libby looked down at the comic, trying to recall the exact memory. Almost a year had passed since the day she'd first met Ginny. So much had happened since then that it felt like she and Ginny had been friends all their lives ....

"You ...," Libby paused, recalling that last bit, "you were holding a newspaper package!"

Chapter 5

Ginny arched an eyebrow.

Libby looked from Ginny to the comic. "*This* was your package?"

Ginny shrugged. "I was hoping to sell it for some cash to supplement my escape fund. I already knew the Snookles were no good, even though I'd just been placed with them. Well, the next day after school, when those bratty nephews of the Snookles were picking on me in the woods and you followed us and ran them off with your slingshot, I remembered that comic. Actually, it was those boys I tried to sell it to the day before! And when you shot them with those purple berries, it was so awesome! I told you at the time that you were my super hero, remember?"

Libby nodded, completely stunned.

"Well, just like how you always keep a slingshot and some purple berries in that backpack of yours, just in case they might come in handy again, *I've* kept this ever since as a reminder that ... well, that good people exist in this world," Ginny's chubby, freckled face bobbed enthusiastically as she spoke. "And when your birthday was coming up, I kept wondering what I could get for you. Then I remembered my comic book. I think this one is perfect for you! Especially now, since you've found out about your, um, your witch-ness ...."

Libby riffled through the comic, desperate to understand Ginny's meaning. Bright, dramatic pictures of Spiderman splashed over the pages, but she didn't understand what any of that could possibly have to do with her ....

"Oh, for goodness sakes, kid," huffed Sal. "Get it? Spiderman was just some geeky teen who got bit by a radioactive spider and suddenly had all these powers he didn't know what to do with."

"*With great power comes great responsibility!*" chimed Uncle Frank.

"But then he learns to use his powers for good—he learns how to *develop* them," added Ginny.

"And he saves a lot of people, blah-blah-blah," said Sal.

"See?" Ginny grinned. "Totally you, Libby."

"But I haven't saved anyone," Libby protested before she could stop herself. "I mean, I don't know how to do anything with my powers. I feel totally useless."

"Well that's the point!" said Ginny. "You've got to learn, like Spidey!"

Libby couldn't help but laugh, despite the heaviness she felt inside.

"Thank you, Ginny," she said, giving her a big hug. "I love it. And I'm really glad you didn't sell it, because that would mean you'd probably have run away, and then I'd never have met my best friend!"

Ginny beamed. "Exactly."

"All this hugging and friendship stuff is making me sick," grunted Sal. "Even the wind's disgusted. It's dead as a doornail out here."

Libby glanced at the sails.

Sal was right: they were hanging limp on the masts, with only the occasional flutter to indicate any breeze at all. The water had calmed, too, so that the boat's bow sat still and level to the horizon. From where she stood, Libby could see the canoes approaching, now vaguely able to make out people in each one, their long, dark hair glistening in the sunlight.

For whatever reason, she wondered if the resort they were headed to was some kind of spa—the kind where they make

Chapter 5

their own fancy scrubs and facial treatments—and the idea of Sal getting a facial almost made her laugh out loud.

"Okay, no more sentimental stuff," she promised. "So, what about those moonstones, Uncle Frank?"

Uncle Frank didn't reply at first; he remained at the wheel, pulling handles and adjusting valves until the sails lowered on the masts. After a moment he stopped and looked around. His eyes rested on the horizon to the west, his expression far away when he said:

"Considering our present circumstance, I'm unsure where to begin …."

"Don't worry," growled Sal. "There's nothing like a solid teleportation to prime an audience for the improbable."

"But what if I told you there was a lot more history behind those moonstones than you know, McCool?"

Sal sneered and tapped the side of his left temple. "You may be going senile old man, but this noggin' is a steel trap. I remember *exactly* what our ground crewman Lam told us back in the day: that the stones were passed down in his family from generation to generation; that he'd given them to us because he had no family left to give them to!"

Uncle Frank nodded, his gaze returning to the sea. "But what you don't know is that someone else came looking for them just before Lam's death. You don't remember because you were out. With … Sofia, I believe."

Sal's eyes squeezed into slits. "I've had it up to here with your grudge over that woman! Will I ever live it down, I ask you? What's a man got to do around here to leave the past in the past?"

"Funny you should ask," replied Uncle Frank quietly.

"Because that's exactly what this gentleman came to talk about. The past, that is, not Sofia."

"How do you mean?"

"I mean this man claimed …." Uncle Frank paused, then looked straight at Sal. "Well, he claimed he'd come *from* it."

Chapter 6

The Wizard of Qingdao

That definitely got everyone's attention. Even Buttercup wobbled over, followed by two more visiting seabirds. These birds were smaller than the albatross had been, mostly white, with black-tipped wings and black around the eyes, too.

"Booby birds." Uncle Frank pointed at Buttercup's new friends. "I think those are Masked Boobies, if I recall correctly. Huge range in tropical waters."

One of them made a funny, squawking noise that Buttercup tried to mimic.

"The moonstone," reminded Libby, anxious to hear Uncle Frank's explanation before he got completely sidetracked. "What about it and this guy who visited you?"

Uncle Frank took a deep breath and looked off again. Libby followed his gaze, watching as the canoes approached.

"It is something that has haunted me," he resumed after a moment, almost as if he were speaking to himself. "And I don't know quite how to start …."

"Try the beginning," grumbled Sal.

"That's the problem, because the *beginning*, according to what this guy told me, started over two thousand years ago. That's where—or rather *when*—he claimed to have come from. In his time, he was known as a wizard; a sage who knew the secrets to immortality …."

"Wait a minute!" exclaimed Libby, tearing her gaze from the canoes back to Uncle Frank. She tucked some loose hair behind her ear, watching him very closely. "You're saying that this wizard who visited you way back in the 1930s …."

"We were in Burma with the Flying Tigers in the 1940s, Libby," corrected Uncle Frank. "I'm not *that* old."

"Fine," she said, thinking it would be impolite to point out that, any way you looked at it, Uncle Frank was officially ancient. "You're saying that this *same* guy who visited you in the 1940s … was literally from *two thousand years ago?*"

"As I said, it sounds …."

"Bat-winged-crazy," finished Sal.

"But what does any of this have to do with the moonstone?" pressed Ginny, leaning closer.

"Well, it was this wizard—he called himself Sheng—he said that he was the one who first shared the secret of the moonstone's power." Uncle Frank's voice sounded distant somehow, as though he existed for a moment inside his own memory, the gravelly bass of his voice coming from long, long ago.

"It's a fascinating story," he continued, "one that has to do

Chapter 6

with an emperor who came to see the wizard Sheng, seeking eternal life. Long story short, after meeting with Sheng, this emperor had the moonstone taken from its place in the Himalayas, carved out the heart of it and used it as some kind of power source for an elaborate underground city built for his afterlife."

"Cake-is-ready!" called Esmerelda from the cabin door, but everyone was too caught up in Uncle Frank's story to notice.

Ginny settled onto bench at the starboard side, just across from where Uncle Frank sat at the wheel. "But you're saying this happened thousands of years ago," she stated slowly, as if processing his words. "So how did your friend Lam end up with these stones if they were part of some ancient burial thing?"

"Because it was Lam's ancestor who stole the moonstone from the mausoleum," answered Uncle Frank. "Sheng explained that a terrible curse accompanied the moonstone as a result—that Lam himself remained in danger. So long as a relation of the thief held the stone in his possession, the emperor's spirit would follow their pull, wreaking havoc on the owner *and* on the souls of his ancestors. From what I gather, one of Lam's forefathers carved the stone into three pendants, perhaps hoping to avoid this curse."

Ginny's huge brown eyes watched Uncle Frank, unblinking. "Holy Macaroni," she whispered. "That's, like, something out of a story book!"

"And that," snorted Sal, "is exactly what this malarkey is all about. Pure fiction!"

"I thought so, too," agreed Uncle Frank. "In any case, according to Sheng, when Lam's ancestor stole the moonstone from the tomb all those years ago, the life force of the mausoleum was frozen. Over two thousand years have passed while the emperor's underground city waits in darkness, waiting for the moonstone to return and bring it to life."

The sound of these last words seemed to float in the air around them, filling the space about the deck with an eerie feel, as if the ghosts of Lam's ancestors had awakened from the sound of Uncle Frank's story and now swept invisibly between the masts, waiting for him to finish the tale of their fate.

"I-do-declare!" huffed Esmerelda, stomping toward the wheel. "Do-you-want-to-eat-cake-or-don't-you?"

No one seemed to hear her.

"So," Ginny said as she cleared her throat and looked around her with unease, "the reason this Sheng wizard came to you was because …?"

"Because the emperor's spirit will not rest until the moonstone is returned to its rightful place," answered Uncle Frank. "I guess Sheng figured it was his duty to set things right. He said he'd approached Lam about it before coming to me—that he'd followed the power of the moonstones' pull. Anyway, I'm ashamed to say I didn't exactly pay as much attention as I should have to his story. In fact, it took years for me to see the truth."

"Well-I-do-not-see-what-any-of-that-has-to-do-with-your-contraption-downstairs," Esmerelda replied testily, her little head moving in short, jerky motions. "That-is-what-you-were-supposed-to-explain-was-it-not?"

Libby would have laughed if she were not feeling so bewildered. Because Esmerelda was absolutely right. How Uncle Frank got off on this tangent about Lam and Sheng and some emperor's underground city had nothing to do with the smashed-up teleportation device downstairs.

Sometimes, Libby mused, it takes a robot to point out the obvious.

Chapter 6

"It has everything to do with the contraption downstairs," Uncle Frank said. "I just haven't gotten to it yet."

"Well, then get to it!" snapped Sal. "Because so far, everything you've told us sounds like a bunch of superstitious nonsense that's giving us all the heebie-jeebies. And in a few more minutes, I'm fixin' to hop on one of those canoes and hit a luau, so if you want to do some explaining, you'd better get going!"

Libby looked from Sal to the water and noted that the canoes were drawing closer. Sunlight glinted off smooth ripples in the distance as the paddles crawled in and out of the water in synchronicity, making the canoes look like a troupe of giant, floating centipedes with paddles for legs. The distant sound of chanting voices kept perfect rhythm with the paddle strokes.

Uncle Frank raised a hand in resignation. "Do you remember that café we used to go to in Burma?" he asked, glancing over at Sal. "The one with the tabletops made from chess boards?"

"Of course I remember!" Sal tapped his head. "How many times do I have to say it? Steel trap!"

"Then you'll remember that night," replied Uncle Frank. "It was hot and raining buckets, so we went to the café for a while—it was probably less than a week before the ambush that took Lam's life. You met up with Sofia and some friends, then left early while I played *sittuyin*—Burmese chess. Remember?"

Sal only rolled his eyes in response.

"Well, the man I was playing," continued Uncle Frank, "turns out, was none other than this wizard Sheng guy. I didn't know it at first—I just thought he was some random patron like the rest of us. We played for hours until he finally beat me. Shocked me, to be honest, so I asked him how he'd gotten to be so good at the game. That's when he told me who he was. Said he could sense the power of my moonstone—and then he began to tell me the story I just told you ... among other things."

Libby frowned, trying to block out the swelling rhythm from the canoes; it was so distracting, and their bizarre chants only seemed to magnify Uncle Frank's creepy story.

"So," she noted as matter-of-factly as possible, "I'm wearing a magical moonstone necklace that a wizard from two thousand years ago still wants. Could we get to what this has to do with your machine?"

Uncle Frank nodded. "After I confronted Sheng about the impossibility of his age, he brought up all these theories about movement through time and space—ideas that fall under what we now call quantum mechanics. From what he told me, I later concluded that his ... er, longevity ... had more to do with *that* than actually having lived for thousands of years. In other words, Sheng wasn't actually thousands of years old; he'd just traveled *from* two thousand years ago."

Libby gripped the moonstone with both hands and stared hard at it. "Are you saying," she said slowly, "that you actually *believe* this guy really *traveled through time?*"

"Well, he claimed to have just teleported from a part of China that is now known as Qingdao," replied Uncle Frank, his voice sounding almost as incredulous as Libby's. "So if I believe anything, it's that he didn't just travel through *time*; he traveled through time *and* space."

For a moment, no one spoke, the sound of Uncle Frank's words electrifying the air about them, so much so that the skin on Libby's arms shivered with a tingly, static sensation. Without thinking, she dropped the stone she'd been holding, letting it swing freely from the chain about her neck.

"Sheng claimed that the two were inextricably linked—like

Chapter 6

yarns woven together to create a single cloth," Uncle Frank explained after a moment. "We chatted for hours about theories I'd only brushed against in my studies. Remember, this was in the 1940s. Back then, the whole idea of space-time travel was a fun concept, but I didn't put much stock in it. It was just a relief to hold a conversation with someone whose attention span extended beyond the capacity of a dodo bird." He flicked a sour look Sal's way, but Sal was busy squinting over the water, now hollering "Ahoy, there!" at the approaching canoes.

"Anyway," Uncle Frank continued, "he wrote out all these equations, things about traversable worm holes, electromagnetic fields and …." He paused and, for a split second, his gaze rested on Libby, a troubled expression flitting in those deep, warm eyes.

"Well, he showed me enough to plant the seed of possibility somewhere in this rock-head of mine," Uncle Frank summarized. "He claimed to be living proof that space-time travel wasn't just a theory, but a reality. I dismissed him as crazy at the time, but years later, something extraordinary happened that turned my opinions around—an archeological discovery. I remember the exact date, in fact. After that, I recalled those theories as well as other information Sheng had shared, and that's when I began my project on the contraption below. Time travel is beyond me still, but after tinkering with Sheng's theories for decades, I thought I finally had a handle on the space part, or, as we've been calling it, teleportation …."

The chants from the canoes grew so loud that they drowned Uncle Frank out, and when Libby looked up, she was surprised to find the boats only a few hundred feet away.

"Guys?" she called, raising her voice above the din. "Do they look, like … not-so-welcoming?"

"They look plenty welcoming to me!" cackled Sal.

Libby kept her eyes peeled on the canoes as Sal waved at them enthusiastically. They were so close now, she could see every occupant.

Men rowed most of the canoes, but women stood in the middle of each—except for two older men and a few children interspersed here and there. Some wore long-sleeved garments, but a few of the women were decidedly less clothed. In fact, as far as Libby could tell, it looked like all they had on were strange, grass or mat-like skirts and then … well, their long hair and strategically placed wreaths were the only things that kept them covered on top.

"Oh my goodness!" squeaked Ginny. She'd scrambled from her bench and now stood with Libby on the port side of the ship. "Are we headed to a nudist colony or something?"

"That's the least of our worries," said Uncle Frank, but Libby could barely hear him over the thrum of chants and the *swoosh-swoosh-swoosh* of paddles. "Girls, why don't you two take Esmerelda and Buttercup below deck for a moment? I—"

"Watch out!" yelped Sal, interrupting Uncle Frank as he dove face-first to the deck. "They've got a blunderbuss!"

Just as Sal hit the ground, a blast of gunpowder exploded in the air, followed by a terrifying roar. And then, before Libby could even process what had happened, a million dark objects whizzed toward them.

Chapter 7

Storm of Stones

"They're throwing rocks!" cried Ginny, crawling over the deck toward the cabin door. "What kind of resort *is* this?"

BOOM! Went another blast of gunpowder.

CRACK! A volley of stones smashed against the mainmast just as Ginny scrambled down the cabin stairs.

"Libby, get in the cabin!" shouted Uncle Frank, but Libby stood frozen by the guardrail, her eyes flicking from the canoes to the island beyond, now noticing another fleet of boats leaving the shore. She stared again at the canoes before them, watching as the women hurled stone after stone, clouding the air with rocks that now resembled a flock of attacking birds. And in that exact moment, the strangest thing happened:

As the rocks rained toward them, everything slowed down so that Libby felt she could almost reach out and touch each one … or rather, not touch directly, but somehow push the air *around* the rocks away, like Styrofoam floats in a pool. In fact, it was as if she were doing exactly that, only her hands didn't move—it was with her *eyes*, like her thoughts could create a current, sending the stones floating backward.

"We get it! We're under siege!" screamed Ginny, poking her face through the cabin door. She waved something that looked like one of Sal's white undershirts in the air. "We surrender! Just put some clothes on and stop …."

THWACK!

"Crud!" yelped Ginny. She ducked below deck as more rocks crashed into the cabin door.

Libby didn't even flinch from the commotion; she stood perfectly still and concentrated on moving the rocks away from everyone on deck with her eyes, hardly aware of the screaming and splintering and exploding sounds all around. Then she turned to the canoes, watching them as if in a trance. One of the old men held an ancient-looking shotgun; he was shoving something down the barrel while a girl, probably not much older than Libby, helped hold the gun steady. That must be the thing Sal called a blunderbuss, considered Libby. The gun had a long, brass barrel that widened into a bellow at the opening, like a trumpet.

Libby glanced from the blunderbuss to the women in the nearest canoe as the attackers yelled words she could not understand. The women were shockingly beautiful, but their obvious rage made them terrifying at the same time; their long, dark hair flashed in the sunlight and their eyes were fierce and brave, their teeth gritted with determination as they roared and shouted and pummeled the *Liberté* with rocks.

Every now and then, a discernable word could be heard,

Chapter 7

although it definitely wasn't English, but the word was shouted over and over, as if it were poison spat from their mouths:

"Papalangi!"

All around, rocks smashed and zoomed, exploding like thunder against water and metal and wood.

"Libby!" cried Uncle Frank, just as Libby felt her midsection tugged away. Uncle Frank had her by the waist and was carrying her toward the cabin as his mobile unit's spider-legs click-click-clicked over the deck and a blizzard of stones whizzed past.

BOOM! Went another volley of stones against the ship deck.

"McCool! Esmerelda! Where's Buttercup?" cried Uncle Frank.

"Got 'em!" came Sal's voice from the other side of the cabin. He stumbled down the steps, followed by an indignant Esmerelda, who was chattering things like "I-do-declare!" and "This-is-most-unacceptable!"

POW! Another cloud of gunpowder mushroomed in the air just as Uncle Frank slammed the cabin door shut behind them.

"We've got to get out of here before those lunatics rip a hole in our boat!" panted Uncle Frank.

"Or before they climb aboard!" added Sal.

"But there's no wind!" wailed Ginny, twisting the white undershirt in her hands. "And besides, how else are we going to get to that resort …?"

"Ginny, there *is* no resort!" snapped Uncle Frank. "Now, help me with that panel over there—the one with the red and blue switches, okay?"

It wasn't until then that Libby saw the trickle of red coming from Uncle Frank's forehead.

"Uncle Frank, you've been hit!"

"Don't you worry about that; it's just a scratch—nicked me good their first volley. Are you sure you didn't get hurt?" he asked, looking her up and down. "I don't know how we didn't get stoned to death up there!"

Libby followed his gaze, still stunned from the attack. She didn't feel hurt at all—nothing but the lump on her forehead from this morning.

"Kid, you were just standing there!" added Sal, inspecting a welt on his arm. "Frye's right—you were in the midst of it—as cool as a cucumber!"

"What do you want me to do with the panel?" yelled Ginny from beyond the galley, bringing everyone's attention back to the present. Uncle Frank clicked over to a steering wheel that sat almost directly below the one on deck.

"See those two blue switches?" he called, pushing open a wooden slide that had covered a narrow window above the steering wheel. Then he bent under the wheel, his mobile unit whirring as it lowered to the floor. "Flick them up when I say so."

"Those-stones-flew-all-around-us," Esmerelda noted as Uncle Frank tinkered with something under the wheel. "It-is-almost-like-an-invisible-force-field-had—"

"Now!" shouted Uncle Frank.

WUH-WUH-WUAH-BWAAAA

An engine sputtered to life from the bowels of the ship, shaking the cabin with its loud shudders. Uncle Frank grabbed the wheel, flicking more switches on the control panel.

"Woo-hoo!" cackled Sal, pushing away a curtain from an oval window. "Bet they weren't counting on that!"

Libby stumbled over and peered out the window. As water churned in gentle wakes behind the *Liberté*, the men in the canoes fumbled with their oars, the expressions on their faces a mixture of astonishment and fear. The old man with the blunderbuss had disappeared somewhere in the chaos, while a few of

Chapter 7

the children and younger women continued to hurl stones that splashed uselessly into the sea.

"What *was* that?" gasped Libby, still staring out the window at the bewildered canoe-ers. All but two of the women had given up on the rock-throwing at this point; most were covering their ears while some looked up at the sky, as if expecting something to fall from the heavens.

"A diesel engine," grinned Sal. "And I do believe that little addition was *my* idea, by the way. I await your gratitude, Frye!"

Uncle Frank sighed and shook his head, his gaze locked on the view through his narrow windshield. Libby continued to peer through Sal's window, watching as the *Liberté* arced away from the canoes, now heading parallel to the island, plying through the deep, blue sea.

"I guess the fire dancing and luau will have to wait," Ginny muttered, joining them. "So where do we go now?"

"We'll circle around and see if there's anything more inviting beyond," announced Uncle Frank. "The South Pacific is riddled with islands; hopefully, we'll find a friendlier spot before long. I just wish I knew what that attack was all about. Makes no sense whatsoever."

Sal harrumphed in response, which was probably the closest he would ever come, thought Libby, to agreeing with Uncle Frank on anything.

"What was that word they kept shouting?" asked Libby, watching the canoes in the increasing distance.

"*Papalangi*," answered Esmerelda. "My-translation-device-indicates-it-means-foreigner. It-is-a-word-commonly-used-in-Polynesia-but-I-can-not-ascertain-from-the-word-which-country-specifically."

"So they're attacking us because we're *foreigners?*" cried Ginny, her mouth puckering up. "That's prejudiced!"

Uncle Frank raised his wiry eyebrows. "Generally speaking, death-by-stoning does tend to be rather prejudicial."

"Yeah, but, they don't even know who we are! Why do they hate us so much?"

As Ginny spoke, Libby continued looking out the window at the fading forms of the women in the canoes. That same strange feeling of slow motion returned to her for a moment, and she suddenly felt as if her mind could stretch through the Plexiglas of the window and curl through the air like a finger; as if she could almost *touch* the minds of those women in the canoes and feel their thoughts.

"I think it's more like fear," said Libby, scrunching up her face in concentration. "I get the feeling they are ... they're *protecting* something. There's this picture of all these men ...."

"What?"

"Oh! I ...." Libby stopped, forcing her sight from the window to the cabin floor, completely unnerved by what was happening, because just as she'd begun to sense the thoughts of those women outside, random images of male faces had started flashing in her mind, faces she'd never seen before in her life ... until now.

She stared at the floor, but the faces still came and went in her mind, pulsing in and out, changing with the thoughts of the women in the canoes. Some of the men's faces she saw were grim or stoic, some wide-eyed with terror, some beaten so badly that their swollen eyes and mouths could yield little expression. Libby squeezed her eyes shut, trying to make the images go away, because the last thing she needed right now was to hallucinate about imaginary people.

"Well, afraid or not," huffed Ginny, "they've got some serious anger management issues! And speaking of issues, what were you thinking, just standing out there like that? You could've been killed! I mean, you didn't even *move!*"

"I didn't need to," Libby replied distractedly.

Sal snorted. "What in tarnation do you mean, kid?"

"The rocks," she said. "They ... well, it was like you could kind of push them away or something, right? Like ...." She stopped, instantly realizing how ridiculous that sounded.

"I think you'd better lie down, kiddo," said Uncle Frank. "Maybe that bump on your head is a lot worse than we'd thought, but in any case, Ginny's right. It's a miracle none of us was seriously injured, especially you."

Sal held up a stubby finger. "Just one rock, kid. The way those things were flying, just one is all it would've taken and then," he snapped his fingers, "that's all she wrote."

Libby blinked, looking from Sal to Uncle Frank, then to Ginny and Esmerelda. At first, she thought they must all be joking—that slow-motion thing that had happened on deck was impossible not to have noticed; how could they be so blind? But from their grim expressions, it was clear they hadn't seen what *she'd* seen. A chill ran down her back.

"I ... I think I will lie down for a minute," she mumbled, and with that, she walked toward the bunks, feeling frustrated and shaken. She knew she wasn't hallucinating from her concussion. She knew that she *definitely* saw those rocks slow down while she was on deck, but it was also just as clear that, no matter how sure she was of what she'd seen, apparently, she was the only one who had. And that was something she needed to think about.

Because ... what did it *mean?* And if this was a manifestation of one of her powers, how did she get it, and how would she know how to bring it back?

Libby shook her head and sank onto the bottom bunk. She crawled into the corner and brought her knees up under her chin, wrapping her arms around her legs as she thought about this rather unsettling discovery.

Slowing down time was a pretty cool trick, Libby had to admit. But not knowing *how* it had happened … well, it was kind of scary, too. Because if she could slow down hurling rocks without even knowing it, if she could push them away like … well, like a force field, as Esmerelda had said, then what else was she capable of? And what if somehow, sometime down the road, what if these same powers came back, but instead of helping, they hurt? What if she was just as capable of sending rocks *into* people as having them curve around them?

Libby shuddered, wishing more than ever that her mother were here.

"Want to explain what happened out there?" said Ginny, showing up at the bunks. She handed a paper plate with a piece of birthday cake to Libby, then took a bite out of her own. "Like, specifically, what you meant about pushing away rocks and seeing strange men's faces?"

Libby put the plate down and leaned her back against the cabin wall, unsure of what to say. She knew Ginny was only trying to help, but still, if she told her best friend what she was beginning to suspect—that she could slow down time and even maybe, just maybe, get a glimpse of people's thoughts, just like Sabine's book of magic suggested—well … it sounded an awful lot like powers a villain out of one of Ginny's comic books would have ….

"Will you look at *that!*" bellowed Sal's voice.

Libby and Ginny exchanged glances.

"C'mon!" said Ginny, shoving the last bite of cake into her

Chapter 7

mouth before darting out of the room. Libby scrambled from the bunk and ran after Ginny to the stairs, just as Sal flung open the cabin door and clamored onto the deck.

"What is it?" called Libby.

They joined Sal on deck, following his gaze. In the time they'd been below, the *Liberté* had traversed around the island enough for them to see the stretch of horizon on the other side. And over the ripples dancing in sunlight, like something that had sailed straight out of one of those glass bottles found on the bookshelves of old, dusty studies, a large, white ship floated, its two towering masts fluttering huge, square sails.

Sal pointed excitedly at the ship. "You see that brig, too, right? I'm not just seeing things?"

"If by 'brig' you mean a ship," replied Libby, squinting from the sun's glare, "the answer is yes."

"Then I'll be a pickled pig's foot!" Sal whooped, dancing a bow-legged jig that made him look like a bald leprechaun in overalls. He grinned a huge, toothless grin and said, "All we need is five minutes on board with their radio, girls, and then we'll be saved!"

Chapter 8

The Visiting Ship

The sky blazed with golds and reds. Libby watched as the sun slowly dipped below the water, melting its colors over the sea. It reminded her of a scoop of orange sherbet, but maybe that was just because she was hungry. And all around, the breeze whipped up with the smell of salt and a hint of seaweed.

"I'm starving!" exclaimed Ginny, pacing the deck. "How much longer?"

"They said they'd be back before nightfall," Libby reminded Ginny, looking at the visiting ship that floated in the distance. With the help of Uncle Frank's binoculars, she could make out the brig's name: *Leonora* was painted in dark letters against the white hull. Something about that caught her attention, as if, just as she'd seen flashes of faces in the minds of those women

Chapter 8

earlier, beneath the white paint of that ship, she saw something else ... but what?

She lowered the binoculars and looked away, watching Ginny, who was scurrying around the table they'd set up on the deck, re-arranging the medley of tin plates and cups from the cabinets below.

Even though Libby didn't say so, she had to agree with Ginny's impatience. It had already been hours since three men from the brig's rowboat had paid them a visit, so why hadn't the *Leonora* crew invited them on board by now, especially when all Sal needed was to use their radio? And why did those three men insist on bringing a whole meal's worth of food to them instead of just having the *Liberté* crew over for dinner?

Ginny scrunched up her nose. "Are you sure you understood them correctly?" she demanded. "Because all I got from that conversation was *'Arvo mates!'* and then something about *'Avin us over for dinnies.'* I mean, what?"

"It's called Australian, Ginny," chuckled Uncle Frank. "And I'm sure our accents sound just as funny to them."

"Maybe so, but I still think those guys are weird," Ginny persisted. "Did you see the look on that man's face when he saw Esmerelda? I thought he was going to fall overboard from shock!"

"I guess it isn't every day when a fella encounters a talking robot in the South Pacific," Uncle Frank replied, distracted, as he squinted over the horizon. "And you can stop pacing, Ginny," he added. "I think I see them coming now."

They all turned to see a wooden rowboat approaching from the other ship. This time, Libby counted four men on board. She wondered if one of them was the American they'd mentioned earlier, because between all the sailor-slang, she'd picked out something about a "fellow yank" who was—she was pretty sure she'd understood this part correctly—their captain. But then again, they'd also mentioned several crew members who were from England and New Zealand, so it was hard to say. She just hoped *all* of those guys had had a chance to clean up a bit for supper; thanks to their previous visit, she'd already discovered the hard way that sailors on brigs do *not* smell good. More like the world's most toxic blend of onions and garlic ....

"'Bout time!" harrumphed Sal, who had apparently found his dentures because he now sported a full set of teeth. "The sooner we eat and give them the grand tour of this baby, the sooner I can get over there and use their darn radio. Why we're standing on ceremony while we're out in the middle of nowhere is beyond me, but I guess it's better late than never."

"I-suppose-I-will-stay-with-Buttercup-to-avoid-shocking-anyone-else-by-my-mere-existence," said Esmerelda with a funny noise that Libby guessed was supposed to sound like a sniff. The robot turned toward the cabin. "And-if-you-are-to-succeed-in-using-their-radio, Sal, then-I-suggest-being-polite. Which-means-you-should-probably-try-not-to-speak."

Esmerelda walked down the stairs before Sal could reply, calling to Buttercup and saying something about sesame seeds she'd found in the galley cabinet.

Ginny bustled about the table, making last-minute arrangements while Sal flicked a switch to activate a few strings of solar-powered white lights they'd hung overhead, so that the deck looked like a magical, floating restaurant. All that was missing now was the food ....

"Cooee!" called a voice from the water.

Libby and Sal ran to the side and looked over, surprised to find the rowboat already saddled up to them. One of the men

Chapter 8

who had visited before brandished a rope and then tossed it up. Sal caught the end and tied it to a cleat as Libby uncoiled the rope ladder from the guard rail.

"See you've brought the goodies!" Sal smacked his lips and grinned down at the baskets of food in the rowboat, just as a portly man grabbed the rope ladder and scrambled up the links with surprising agility.

Before Sal managed to take one of the baskets of food being hoisted toward him, the portly man was already on deck, smiling as he turned to Libby.

"Good evening!" he said in a booming voice.

Libby blinked up at him in surprise.

While the other sailors had obviously cleaned up a little, this guy had taken it to a whole new extreme; he wore a formal black suit with a starched white waistcoat, and a fancy chain dangled between the lapels of his jacket, curving over his rounded belly. His dark hair was parted and slicked back, his mustache and beard were extremely well-trimmed, and when he smiled, his teeth were surprisingly white ... compared to the other sailors, at least.

"May I introduce myself? I believe we are fellow compatriots," the man continued as he bent to Libby's eye level, and before she realized what was happening, he'd taken her hand and was lifting it to his lips. "My name is Captain Hayes, hailing originally from the great State of Ohio. And you are?"

"Um, Libby!" she answered, yanking her hand away before he could kiss it.

"Sal McCool," said Sal, who, much to Libby's relief, stepped in and was now shaking the captain's hand. "And this is our fearless Captain Francis Phinneus Frye ...." Sal smirked, ignoring Uncle Frank's grimace, "and of course, this is our ... er, Health and Safety Officer, Ginny Gonzalez. We're pleased to have you all on board the *Liberté* ...."

Sal rambled on as the other sailors joined them on deck, but Libby noticed Captain Hayes wasn't really paying attention to anything being said. Rather, he stared at the tiny, white lights twinkling over the dining table. Then, slowly, as if in a daze, the captain took in the rest of the deck, pausing whenever he met with one of Uncle Frank's inventions. He turned to the metal pipes that ran from the deck to the masts overhead.

"You're using sail *and* steam power?" he asked, pointing to the pipes.

"Why, indeed, yes!" Uncle Frank rolled the wheels of his mobile unit toward the captain. Libby noticed that, for some reason, Uncle Frank had taken to using the wheel-chair mode over his spider legs or even the occasional hover-vent elevation device—maybe, she considered, to avoid overwhelming their visitors? She wasn't sure.

"It powers the mechanics for the sails and whatnot," continued Uncle Frank. "Cuts down on manpower, obviously; there's no way we'd manage this ship otherwise."

"I've read about that idea," replied Captain Hayes in a thoughtful voice, walking past Uncle Frank and standing closer to the masts. "And these ... surfaces," he continued, pointing to the solar panels. "What on earth are they?"

"Solar panels, of course!" said Ginny, joining the captain by the mast. "Uncle Frank made those, too. He's a genius!"

"I see that he is," murmured the captain.

Sal snickered and slapped him on the back.

"Hayes, I do believe you've been at sea a tad too long. Frye's got as many alternative energy sources as mankind can think of ... short of nuclear, I'd venture, although I wouldn't

Chapter 8

be entirely surprised to discover a miniature nuke plant on this clunker somewhere ...."

"Yes, of course!" agreed Captain Hayes. He frowned at the ground, as if deep in thought, but when he looked up again, that same, bright smile stretched across his face. He gestured to one of his men. "Now, Cal, you've got that grog we brought? It's rude to keep our hosts waiting."

The sailor called Cal stumbled forward, holding large, ceramic jugs in each hand, his eyes glued to the metal windmill on top of the main cabin that had suddenly came to life from a gust of wind, its blades twirling merrily.

"Blimey," he muttered.

"You will have to excuse us," said the captain, leveling a hard stare Cal's way as he took the jugs and placed them on the table. "It has been a while since we've encountered such company, as our manners may have betrayed. Now, John and Hamish, set the food on the table, would you? And Cal, shut your mouth before the flies settle in."

Uncle Frank chuckled, then scooted to the table and asked the men to make themselves comfortable. But the sailors were so distracted by the white lights overhead that they nearly missed their chairs.

"Heat exhaustion," explained the captain, lifting his eyebrows apologetically.

And with that, dinner began.

Libby hadn't realized how hungry she was—burned fish and super-salty meat and stale bread had never tasted so good! And, turns out, fresh coconut water was pretty delicious. Libby and Ginny drank two coconuts a piece, but their guests seemed more enthralled by the pitchers of fresh water on the table. They kept shaking their heads and declaring that it hadn't rained for days—so how on earth did they have *containers* of the stuff?

Uncle Frank took this as an opportunity to explain his salt water conversion device, but it was clear they didn't understand a word of what he said. And as the sky grew darker and the white lights twinkled overhead, the sailors aboard the *Liberté* poured cup after cup of grog while Uncle Frank chatted and Sal stuffed his face.

"This place is weirder than the Bermuda Triangle," whispered Ginny after a while. "Have you ever seen Uncle Frank talk so much?"

"It's his weakness. Asking him about inventions and scientific theories is like putting a kid in a candy store. If we don't stop him, he'll talk all night long."

"Well, if he keeps going through those jugs of water, sooner or later he's gonna have to stop long enough to pee," noted Ginny.

They both glanced at Uncle Frank, who was now discussing the Heisenberg Uncertainty Principle with increasing enthusiasm while the sailors and Captain Hayes feigned interest and drank more grog. Sal, on the other hand, had managed to eat half the food on the table, and was now enjoying a post-dinner nap.

"I don't like this," muttered Libby. "Sal's content and Uncle Frank's a chatterbox. Everything is upside down."

"Girls, why don't you get us that cake your uncle mentioned?" boomed a voice. Libby and Ginny both jumped and looked up, suddenly realizing that Captain Hayes was staring straight at them. "Unless, of course, you'd rather my men help you …."

"No, no—we'll get it," replied Libby, practically falling out

Chapter 8

of her seat. She grabbed Ginny's arm and walked toward the cabin as briskly as possible.

"Why should we share our cake, just because they brought us some moldy bread?" hissed Ginny under her breath. "And why haven't we been invited on board to use their radio yet? There's something …."

"Fishy?" suggested Libby as she opened the door.

"Definitely."

Libby locked the door behind them as soon as they were both inside. They walked down the stairs in silence and found Esmerelda pacing the galley floor, her little metal hands on her hips. Buttercup sat curled in the corner, his head tucked under a wing.

"Esmerelda, what is it?" whispered Libby.

"I-have-been-asking-myself-that-same-question," she replied, straightening her arms as she turned to them. "I-can-hear-that-conversation-upstairs-and-something-is-amiss. Nobody-is-*ever*-that-interested-in-Frank-Frye's-theories."

Libby nodded in agreement as she sank into the built-in bench.

"What should we do?" said Ginny.

"I-have-an-idea." Esmerelda walked to a cabinet, pushed aside a box of crackers and a plastic jar of Sal's peanut butter, then pulled out a glass bottle that looked remarkably like the herbal tincture Libby's mother would make for Uncle Frank's insomnia. "He-left-this-here-last-weekend, but-it-is-empty."

Libby frowned as she stared at the bottle. "Okay … so you're worried we'll have a cranky, sleep-deprived genius on our hands?" she guessed. "What's that got to do with the sailors upstairs?"

Esmerelda looked back at her with those serene, glassy-grey

eyes, and there was something in her stare that made Libby's pulse pick up. "You-need-to-make-more."

"What?"

"We-will-serve-the-cake-to-those-men," Esmerelda said impatiently, "once-we-have-spiked-it-with-sleeping-potion."

"You can't spike the cake!" cried Ginny. "I *love* that cake!"

"Shhh!" said Esmerelda.

"So then we'll *literally* have a wasted cake and a *whole ship* of sleepy sailors!" Ginny protested, raising her hands in the air. "I thought robots were supposed to be logical!"

"I don't get it," agreed Libby, trying to keep her voice low as she took the bottle from Esmerelda and placed it on the table. "Besides the fact that I don't have the ingredients to make more, even if I knew how, what good would it do?"

"It-will-buy-us-some-time."

"For what?"

"I-normally-have-the-benefit-of-connecting-to-satellite-for-additional-information," replied Esmerelda, shaking her head in frustration, "but-I-do-know-these-men-are-not-who-they-seem. We-need-to-call-for-help-before-things-go-very-wrong."

"Our communication equipment is dead," Ginny reminded the robot with a glare.

"True," said Esmerelda, "but-*they*-have-a-radio."

"On their *ship!*" said Ginny.

"Finally-you-are-catching-on!"

"Oh, wow," Libby murmured. She stood up, feeling her knees wobble under her as the meaning behind Esmerelda's words sank in.

"This makes sense to you?" demanded Ginny.

Libby nodded, swallowing down the fear that tightened her throat, because as farfetched as Esmerelda's idea was, she knew the little robot was right. She turned to Ginny. "You saw the way they were looking at our boat," she said, her voice low but urgent, "like they were calculating what everything's worth. And don't you think it's strange they waited 'til evening to come aboard when they've had all day to visit?"

Ginny didn't reply, but as Libby spoke, their situation—and what she had to do about it—grew increasingly clear. "That means *you* have to distract them with the cake," she continued, "while *someone else* sneaks to the brig to use the radio …." Libby paused to swallow hard, suddenly feeling like she had a whole coconut stuck in her throat. "And that someone, I'm pretty sure …." She paused again to look at Esmerelda.

"Go-on, Liberty-Frye."

"Well…." Libby gulped, hardly believing what she was about to say. "Well, that *someone* has to be me!"

Chapter 9

The Substitute Potion

"Wait a minute! Wait a minute!" Ginny raised her hands to her head. "We're not—what do you—you can't—*WHAT?*"

"Esmerelda's right," said Libby, feeling certain now that she'd said it. "Sal's ... well, he's out of commission. And Uncle Frank's so caught up in everyone's pretend-attention that he doesn't realize what's happening, not to mention the obvious fact that he can't exactly hop on a dinghy and then sneak onto a ship with that mobile unit of his. So that leaves the three of us. Esmerelda certainly can't go—she'd never even make it to the deck without raising the alarm. I mean, you saw the way those sailors stared at her earlier. And Dad's given me a few lessons before, so I think I can handle the rowboat—the brig's not that far away—"

Chapter 9

"It's the *MIDDLE OF THE NIGHT!*" wheezed Ginny, her eyes widening to the size of two full moons. "In the *SOUTH PACIFIC!*"

"You-have-a-talent-for-stating-the-obvious."

"And what makes you think you can sneak on that ship better than a robot, anyway?" continued Ginny, ignoring Esmerelda.

"Well, I won't short-circuit if I fall into the water, for starters." Libby tried to sound more sure of herself than she felt, because the truth was, she knew Ginny was also right. The idea of sneaking off unnoticed in a rowboat, making it to the brig, sneaking on and then using the radio undetected—if she could even find the thing, not to mention getting the right frequency—was nothing short of ... well, madness.

"But how do we know this is even *necessary?*" persisted Ginny, now waving her hands wildly. "Those guys upstairs are annoying, yes, but they could just be having a good time! That's what sailors do, right? Drink grog and stuff? Especially in the South Pacific—everybody knows that! It's ... it's grog drinking, eye patch wearing, talk-like-a-pirate wacky paradise out here! Robots don't get it! So why should *she* be the expert on what we should do?"

"Because-I-saw-something-on-their-boat," Esmerelda said. "You-know-that-infrared-capability-of-mine? I-used-it. I-could-detect-something-in-the-hold-of-their-ship."

"What's a hold?" asked Libby.

"The-storage-area."

"They said they're copra exporters," snapped Ginny, her face blooming red with impatience. "Which means, as you yourself explained to us, they've got a bunch of dried coconut for cargo! Which means, *of course* their storage area is going to look weird!"

"Hold," corrected Esmerelda.

Ginny rolled her eyes. "Of course their *hold* is going to look weird!"

Now it was Esmerelda's turn to roll her eyes. Except in her case, when they had settled, the pupils were now lenses and a bunch of tiny bulb-looking things took up the space where the glassy grey of her irises had been.

"When-you-open-your-mouth,Ginevieve-Rae-Gonzalez,my-thermographic-sensor-detects-all-that-hot-air-with-a-heat-imprint-of-mostly-orange."

Ginny made a face like she'd just swallowed a whole jug of nasty grog, but before she could muster a reply, Esmerelda continued.

"And-Liberty-Frye, while-you-have-an-aura-that-extends-far-beyond-the-usual, that-necklace-you-have-on-should-be-near-violet, which-is-a-cool-heat-index. But-instead, it-glows-almost-white. White-is-the-hottest-heat-index."

"Fine," said Ginny. "So you see special colors. What's your point?"

"For one, I guess my necklace should be burning a hole in my chest, but it doesn't *feel* hot," muttered Libby, tugging the chain until the moonstone slipped out from under her shirt.

"It's glowing!" exclaimed Ginny, staring in amazement at the amulet. "Just like in Germany, remember? Ours would glow when one of us was in danger!"

"My-*point*," Esmerelda continued, "is-that-dried-coconut-stored-for-weeks-in-the-bowels-of-a-ship-would-produce-no-heat, so-the-heat-imprint-should-be-violet-or-black. And-yet-the-hold-is-filled-with-warm-light. *Moving*-warm-light."

"Yeah," said Ginny, turning back to the robot. "Like maybe there are some sailors down there, actually doing their jobs?"

Chapter 9

"More-like-at-least-twenty-people-jammed-together. And-from-the-heat-signature-around-their-wrists-and-ankles, I-would-guess-they-are-chained."

Ginny drew back in surprise. The silence gave Libby enough time to digest what Esmerelda was saying. It also pulled together all the bizarre thoughts she'd encountered that day, including the unnerving sensation she'd had when she looked at the *Leonora*.

"Those faces I saw earlier, when the women were throwing stones," Libby began slowly, "they were images of men mostly, and some younger boys. They looked afraid; like they were being attacked or held hostage or something …."

Ginny's head snapped up. "Are you thinking that those people … those faces … that they're on the *ship?*"

Libby nodded, equally stunned by the revelation.

For a moment, nobody spoke.

"And … and you're volunteering to go *over* there," wheezed Ginny, "knowing you could end up like the rest of them?"

"Well, I've got to try." Libby cleared her throat, hoping to still the sudden tremor in her voice, and even as the words came out, she knew how insane her plan sounded.

"Look," she persevered, trying to sound confident, "we already know Captain Hayes is up to no good. And now, based on what Esmerelda has seen, the fact that my necklace is glowing and what's going on up there," she jabbed a finger in the direction of the deck, "we can safely assume they're gonna hijack our ship … or something worse. But if I can get to the radio, at least I can call for help before that happens. And you two can tie these guys up or something once they fall asleep!"

Ginny sucked in a sharp breath. "And the heat imprints of the people that Esmerelda saw?"

"I'll report that, too, of course. The trick is finding the radio before the crew over there finds me. And I need to do it soon because the longer we hold off on our plan, the more likely the rest of those sailors are going to come for us!"

"What about Uncle Frank and Sal?"

Libby and Esmerelda exchanged glances.

"Well," Libby answered uneasily, "we'll have to serve them the cake, too, or else it'll look suspicious …," she trailed off.

Ginny exhaled loudly. "I guess we don't have a choice," she said after another moment, her voice gaining confidence. "We should get started then. Libby, hurry up and do your thing with the sleeping potion! And when you're done, we'll need to lock Buttercup in the cabin so he doesn't follow you to the other ship!"

Libby stared down at the empty bottle on the table. With all that had just happened, she'd forgotten all about the first step of Esmerelda's plan, and she couldn't believe she was actually having this thought, but the idea of sneaking off all alone in a rowboat in the middle of the Pacific and then sneaking on board an enemy ship anchored somewhere out there in the darkness suddenly felt a lot less intimidating than conjuring a sleeping potion.

"But I *told* you," she finally managed to reply, "I don't have the ingredients!"

"So improvise," Ginny said. "Tick tock, Libby. Time's a-wasting."

"But I don't even know how! I mean, my mom's the one who makes that potion for Uncle Frank. I've only glanced at the recipe a few times—"

"Libby," Ginny cut in sternly, crossing her arms. "Now is not the time to back out of this. Remember Spiderman?

Chapter 9

With great power comes great responsibility! So practice your magic already."

"But I don't have the ingredients!"

"Just substitute; like in baking, you can use apple sauce instead of oil. Do something like that!"

"But I'm not making banana bread!" cried Libby in exasperation. "You don't just ad-lib a spell, Ginny! It's dangerous! Really, really bad things can happen!"

Ginny pressed her mouth together as she shook her head from side to side. Then she said, "You've got your spell book and you've got those purple berries in your backpack, I know that you do. Surely you can make something with that! It doesn't have to be *exactly* like your mom's herbal tincture—"

"It won't be a *thing* like my mom's herbal tincture because I DON'T HAVE THE INGREDIENTS!"

"Purple berries can do all sorts of things," continued Ginny, as if not hearing her friend. "I speak from experience. I mean, if they practically raised your parents from the dead, surely they can do a little thing like put some rowdy sailors to sleep."

Libby groaned, then looked to Esmerelda for support, but the little robot only raised her shoulders and blinked back at her. Libby took a few deep breaths, forcing herself to calm down. For better or worse, she knew she had to do *something*, and she had to do it fast. Captain Hayes would start wondering what the delay was if they stayed down here much longer ….

With her heart pounding in her chest, she walked over to the bunks, grabbed her bag from the bottom bed and then carried it into the galley, the whole time feeling as if her knees had dropped from her legs. She took Sabine's little book out of her bag and thumbed through the pages with trembling fingers. Silently, she told herself that following a potion recipe from

Sabine's magic book was a lot easier than the more abstract arts like mind-listening or conjuring ….

But what if something horrible happens? she couldn't help but worry. *I've never made a potion for human beings to actually drink before. What if I turn everyone into frogs or something, like in the fairy tales? Or send Uncle Frank into a coma?*

Libby searched through her book, looking for something less drastic.

"Well, this one's the closest I can get," she decided out loud as she stopped on a page halfway through. Her voice shook so much that she had to clear her throat, and it felt like everything in the galley area was suddenly floating around her. She tried to focus on the words before her eyes.

"So," she continued, reaching for a saucepan from the cabinet and holding it tight to hide her trembling hands, "let's cut up one berry, then bring a cup of water to a rolling boil and …," she paused to squint at the list of ingredients, her heart falling into her stomach when she saw what came next, "… is there anything we can substitute for *widgewood?*"

Chapter 10

Feathers and Fate

Thirty minutes later, the entire deck of the *Liberté* resounded with snores.

Well, almost.

Uncle Frank tottered a bit in his mobile unit, his eyes opening and closing blearily.

"Are you sure this stuff is just supposed to put you to sleep?" asked Ginny, staring in fascination at the sailor named Hamish. Unlike Cal, John and Captain Hayes, who lay in various unflattering positions on the floor, Hamish sat straight up in his chair with both hands palms down on the table, and if it weren't for his occasional snoring, Libby would have thought he was practicing some sort of South Seas meditation.

She looked around the deck, hardly believing that the spell had actually worked, especially considering the substitute she'd had to make. Then she glanced anxiously to the cabin door, where Esmerelda was dragging four coils of rope up the stairs in a not-so-stealthy fashion.

Libby cringed at the racket, knowing she should head for that rowboat before anyone woke up, but she couldn't bear to leave Uncle Frank like this.

"I'm so sorry, Uncle Frank," she whispered in his ear as she leaned over him. "Please don't be mad; Esmerelda and Ginny will be here to watch over you. They're gonna tie up the bad guys while I'm away, and I'll be back as soon as I can!"

Uncle Frank tried to grab her arm, but his hand fell feebly to his lap. "No, Libby!" he wheezed. "The machine downstairs ... and Captain Hayes—"

A loud snore from Hamish's direction cut Uncle Frank off and was followed by a strange spasm that shook the whole table. Libby glanced over to see the sailor now slumped over the table, his arms twitching in the oddest way, and while Libby couldn't be sure, it almost looked like something white was stuck to his forehead.

"I'd better get going before he wakes up," Libby worried under her breath.

"Oh, no, boogley bear, please don't go," came another voice.

Libby whipped around in time to see Ginny giggling as she pointed at the sailor named John. He lay curled on his side, deep in sleep, grinning with his arms wrapped around his own waist. "Please, Bonnie-Bee, give us a kissy-wissy."

"Or before I throw up," Libby added, but just then she felt her backpack tugged with surprising strength, and she turned to see Uncle Frank staring at her.

"Please, Libby ...," he persisted, his voice strained with desperation, but even as he spoke, his eyes drooped heavy with

Chapter 10

sleep. "You need to know ... our communication equipment ... anything run by satellite—"

"Don't worry, Uncle Frank," she replied quickly, trying to soothe him, "I'm going to the other ship to find their radio. Soon, we'll be rescued and everything will be okay!"

Uncle Frank's eyes widened in horror, his lips parting as if to speak, but then, in the next moment, his head slumped down, chin against chest. Seconds later, his snores told Libby all she needed to know.

She kissed the top of his head, swallowing down the guilt swelling in her throat. She didn't have time for it, because right now, she knew she had to get into that rowboat and then figure out a way to sneak on board the other ship before she came to her senses and realized what a ridiculous, crazy and flat-out stupid thing she was about to undertake.

"Um, Libby," called Ginny from the other side of the table. "You sure this was a sleeping potion, right?"

"Of course it's a sleeping potion!"

"Then I wish you could explain this!"

Libby glanced over at Ginny, and it wasn't until then that she realized what her friend was talking about, because growing from Hamish's forehead and even down his throat was the most curious arrangement of downy, white feathers. And it wasn't just Hamish, either. As she panned the deck of the *Liberté*, she saw John, Cal and even Captain Hayes sporting white feathers in the most unexpected of places.

"Oh," Libby gulped. "I didn't think of that possible side effect."

"What side effect?"

"Um. That this ... er, particular spell was ...."

"WHAT?"

"Well, it was meant for Buttercup." Libby glanced at Sal and Uncle Frank, but thankfully, it looked like they were feather-free. "After the whole Germany incident, Sabine probably suspected he might not sleep well, so she stuck this potion in the book for him—"

"You gave human beings a BIRD SPELL?" interrupted Ginny, her lips puckering in indignation. "What were you *thinking?!*"

Libby drew back and crossed her arms, suddenly feeling defensive. "I was thinking that *someone* kept insisting I come up with a potion; that's what I was thinking!"

"With great power comes great responsibility!" hissed Ginny. "And this is NOT responsible!"

"Well, I hate to break it to you, but I'm not Spiderman! I'm a witch! ... sort of. Anyway, I did the best I could under the circumstances—it was *your* idea to substitute Sal's fiber pills for *widgewood!*"

"They're sprouting *feathers!*"

"I can see that!"

"But-Uncle-Frank-and-Sal-are-fine," called Esmerelda, who was in the process of hog-tying Cal. "Perhaps-the-grog-is-causing-a-reaction."

"I think sprouting feathers qualifies as a lot more than *a reaction!*"

Libby rolled her eyes and walked to the rope ladder. "It isn't a permanent spell," she replied irritably, "so it should wear off before they even notice; and anyway, serves them right!" And with that, she began her descent to the rowboat before her nerves got the better of her.

She had just settled into the boat and was grabbing the paddles when she saw Ginny crawling down the rungs.

"What are you doing? Ginny, go back up!"

Chapter 10

"Are you crazy?" huffed Ginny, landing with an ungraceful *THUNK* inside the boat. She scrambled from the floor to a bench. "I'm not staying here with a bunch of freaky sailors! *Especially* not ones who talk to Bonnie-Bee about kissy-wissies!"

"But it's too dangerous!" hissed Libby. "Besides, what about Uncle Frank and Sal?"

Ginny shook her head so hard that her cheeks jiggled. "Nobody will blame them—they were already out of it before we started drugging everybody. Esmerelda can fend for herself and Buttercup can fly away if he wants! But me?" She wiped her brow, which was uncharacteristically messy. Strands of loose hair stuck to her sweaty skin; in fact, Libby had never seen Ginny's ponytail look so unkempt before. "When they wake up, they'll know it was *me* who did *that* to them. No, thanks!"

Libby frowned, glancing from Ginny to their ship. From here, all she could see were the fading white lights that Sal had strung above the dining area, their glow dimming as the night crawled on. Soon, they would fade altogether, and when that happened, Libby knew she'd be lost in an ocean of darkness.

Literally.

"We don't have time to argue," she decided, grabbing the rope that held the rowboat to the *Liberté*. She untied it from the ring near the bow, making sure there was another rope coiled on the floor first, then lowered the oars into the water.

She pulled at the oars, and as their rowboat gently drifted from the side of the ship, Libby had to admit that having Ginny around was a huge comfort. But at the same time, she felt responsible for her, even worried. What if something went wrong? It was one thing to volunteer your own services for a mission most-likely-to-fail, but dragging your best friend along?

"Why aren't we moving faster?" demanded Ginny, fidgeting

on the boat bench as if trying to find just the right spot on their comfy couch back home. Her movements sent the boat rocking from side to side, which did nothing to help with Libby's queasiness.

Libby concentrated on the rowing, forcing her mind onto the rhythm of pushing out then pulling in, pushing out and pulling in, of breathing in the salt air, of anything other than the fact that she felt like she was about to throw up.

Finally, Ginny settled down so her back was pressed against the side of the boat and her body faced the rest of the bench. She crossed her legs yoga-style, then raised an impatient eyebrow.

"You've got to paddle harder, Libby!"

"Would you like to help?" Libby snapped, unsure whether the sweat popping from her forehead was from the exertion of rowing or from trying not to throw up.

"No, thank you. I'll keep time for you as you obviously need to work on your technique. I think that's best."

"Shocking," muttered Libby, gripping the oars harder.

"So, let's go! One-two, one-two, one-two …."

Libby gritted her teeth as she continued to pull the paddles through the water, thinking she'd definitely been wrong before:

Ginny was *not* a comfort.

"One-two, one-two, one-two …."

Libby grunted and pulled as the rowboat inched across the sea, the current fighting her with every paddle stroke. Her back was to the brig, but she could see the *Liberté* looming in front of her, and it looked way closer than she knew it should. In fact, it looked like they'd hardly moved at all … which probably had something to do with the fact that Ginny wasn't helping.

"One-two, one-two …."

Chapter 10

Pull, push, pull, push. *Just focus on that*, thought Libby. *At least she's not telling me to use my witch ....*

"I have an idea!" cried Ginny, interrupting her count. "You should use your witch powers! Just think about the boat moving faster; think really hard about it and ...."

Sweat dripped from Libby's face as she continued to pull at the oars and Ginny continued to chatter. Despite her efforts, that familiar swell of resentment ballooned inside.

"I mean, I don't see how come you don't know how to do *anything* yet," Ginny continued as she readjusted her position on the bench, sending the rowboat lurching again from side to side. "But I'm glad we have this opportunity to talk about it, actually, because we really do need to get this out in the open."

"Get ...." Libby paused to swallow down another roll of nausea, then pulled harder at the oars. Her arms were already shaking from the strain, but she knew she couldn't stop. It was either get to that brig or be stranded in a little wooden dinghy with a chatty, non-rowing boat mate in the middle of the Pacific. She tried to speak again. "Get ... *what* out in the open?"

"Well, this whole witch business, of course," Ginny replied. She stretched out her arms so they rested against the sides of the rowboat, then extended her legs so she more or less lay across the bench seat. Rolling her head back to gaze at the sky, she sighed contentedly. "It's really quite pretty here, don't you think? I mean, even without any stars. There's something velvety about the air, have you noticed?"

Libby kept rowing, forcing her gaze just beyond Ginny's reclining form as she clamped her jaw tight. She knew if she opened her mouth right now, she'd say something she'd later regret.

Maybe a lot of things.

And she was afraid that if she actually looked straight at her friend, all that balled-up misery inside her just might do something terrible ….

"What I'm trying to say is that you've had *eight months* to study that silly book Sabine gave you!" continued Ginny. "Eight months! And still, after all that, the only magic trick I've seen you do is afflicting those sailors with feathers!"

"They're not *magic tricks,"* Libby panted as she looked up to see the *Liberté* still floating before her. "It's not like I'm pulling rabbits out of hats or even like I've got a magic wand or something, Ginny! This is for *real;* something that has to be understood and practiced—like a language, I guess. Except nobody knows the language and I have to figure it out all by myself!"

"Whatever," said Ginny. "At least you put them all to sleep. And I'll admit that thing you did with the rocks was pretty cool, but that wasn't intentional, was it? Neither were those faces that you saw from the scary ladies. Nothing you do that is actually *magic*—you know, that isn't just following a recipe or something—is ever *on purpose*. Is that normal?"

"I don't think anything about this situation is normal," Libby replied through gritted teeth.

Ginny folded her hands behind her head and continued gazing at the sky. "Well, I don't want to sound judgmental or anything, but it seems to me like you should be making better progress."

Libby grunted as she strained at the oars, her jaw clamped so tight it ached.

"I mean, according to everything we've heard, you're supposed to *not* just have witch abilities, but super-duper witch abilities, right? It's your fate! Isn't that the whole *reason* why

Chapter 10

Zelna tried to take control over you—just to get your powers? So if you're so powerful, why can't you *do* anything?"

Libby felt the heat from her breath, the pounding between her temples, and her face burned as hot as a summer campfire. For just a second, she imagined opening her mouth and watching as a ball of flames roared toward Ginny. She pressed her lips tighter and continued to row.

"I think you're just not trying hard enough," concluded Ginny, and Libby glared at the night beyond them, forcing herself just to row, row, row.

Minutes passed by in silence.

After a while, Ginny yawned, wiggled back to a normal sitting position and then looked around. Almost immediately, she stiffened so that she sat straight as a ruler, her feet falling from the bench to the floor. "Holy Macaroni!"

"What … now?" panted Libby in exhaustion.

Ginny stared back at her, her face so pale she looked like she'd been blasted with white chalk.

"It-it's just what I was telling you!" she finally managed, lifting a shaky finger to something behind Libby. "Libby, you're doing it! We're already there!"

Chapter 11

Captain's Quarters

When Libby turned around, she couldn't believe it. It should be impossible to have crossed that distance in so short of time, especially considering the current.

"Well!" declared Ginny, recovering. "I'm glad I could help. We should have these talks more often!"

Libby blinked at the brig that floated not ten feet away, too incredulous to comment. Then she noticed the shadow of cargo netting about midway down the ship. It draped from the side so that the thick rope netting almost touched the water.

"We need to go there," she whispered, gingerly lowering her oars once more.

A few strokes later, they were beside the net. She grabbed the rope from their rowboat and stood on shaky legs, straining

Chapter 11

over the side until one hand reached the net while the other looped the end of the rope through it.

A few more tugs and then she cinched a knot—just like her dad had taught her—securing their rowboat to the side. Ginny watched all of this with uncharacteristic silence.

"Ready?" whispered Libby, her voice so quiet that it barely carried through the air.

She pointed at the netting, gesturing that she'd climb up while Ginny stayed with the rowboat. Ginny followed the motion, her eyes popping wide in the process. Then she shook her head violently from side to side and began jabbing her fingers this way and that in a flurry of pantomimes. Libby wasn't sure what exactly she was trying to say, but she had the general impression that Ginny did not approve.

Well, they weren't exactly in a position to discuss strategies on how to sneak aboard enemy ships, so Libby decided to just go for it.

She grabbed the rope netting with both hands and began to climb, her pulse picking up tempo as she pulled herself up the loose, slimy links. By the time she'd climbed level with the boat deck, her arms and legs shook from the strain and her heart raced so fiercely that she was sure someone else might hear it.

She peeked over the side.

Except for one sailor who snored away in a nest of nets and ropes, the deck appeared empty.

Libby flung a leg over the wooden rail and crawled over. When her feet met the main deck of the brig, she tried to ignore her wobbling knees and shaking arms. Her first thought was to signal her arrival to Ginny, so she leaned over the side to glance below.

But she wasn't expecting to see what she saw.

Because from where she stood, she spotted Ginny clinging to the netting several feet down, face pressed against the boat's side so that she looked a bit like a giant crab emerging from the sea ... if crabs had white knuckles and messy ponytails and wore orange t-shirts that said "Grammar Rocks" on them.

"Ginny," Libby hissed as loudly as she dared, "go back to the rowboat!"

But Ginny remained splayed across the rope net, face pressed to the side of the boat, obviously too terrified to move.

Libby bit her lip in frustration as she stared down at her friend. She knew that if she crawled down to get her, she wouldn't have enough energy to make it back up, let alone drag a terrified Ginny along. And any minute now, someone might see her standing in plain view and if that happened, it wouldn't do Ginny—or herself—any good.

Libby knew she had to get to the main cabin and she had to get there fast. She scanned the deck once more, squinting through the darkness. While the fading white lights of the *Liberté* still marked its spot in the distance, no lights could be seen at all on the *Leonora*. It was pretty spooky. Even so, Libby was grateful for the protective shadows. She turned and leaned back over the side.

"Okay," she whispered hurriedly down to Ginny, "just hang tight, and I'll be right back!"

Then she tiptoed over the wooden boards toward the deck at the stern, but just as Libby passed the sleeping sailor, a floorboard creaked underfoot. She froze, not daring to breathe as the sailor snorted and smacked his lips, but a few seconds later, his snores resumed.

Libby continued on, her pulse pounding so violently that it was all that she could hear. She passed the mainmast, now

Chapter 11

tip-toeing toward the ladder-like staircase that led to what she hoped was the quarter deck above, just as Esmerelda had described. And if the robot was correct, just below this, Libby should find a doorway leading into the captain's cabin.

Even though Esmerelda had never been on the *Leonora,* of course, her off-line database held enough information about ships to give them a good idea of where Libby should look. And between dissolving Sal's fiber pills in a cup of boiling water and arguing if Sabine's sleeping potion spell should be pronounced *"Heeber-loof-ga-shloofen"* or *"Hiber-lauf-ge-shlaufen,"* all three of them had at least agreed that a ship radio would most likely be found in the captain's quarters—the biggest cabin toward the back of the boat.

A few more breathless steps, and Libby was finally at the cabin door. Suddenly, all of that breath that she'd been holding came out in a dismayed *whoosh*, because it hadn't occurred to her until that exact moment that the cabin door might be locked and, if it was, she'd have to try her luck with another spell. This, of course, did nothing to calm her nerves, not to mention the fact that any spell from Sabine's book would require another bout of rather German-sounding spell words, and the unfortunate thing about German-sounding spell words was this:

They were impossible to say without drawing attention to one's self.

Libby looked around again—from here, she had a clear view of the main deck. Not a sailor could be seen except for the sleeping one by the ropes; a fact she suddenly realized was rather curious. Because if three sailors and their captain were currently snoozing on the *Liberté*, shouldn't this ship have at least two or three sailors on deck keeping watch?

And what about the cabin boy?

Wasn't there always a cabin boy lurking around on these things? Or that short, fat, baldish guy from *Peter Pan* with the striped shirt ... what was his title?

She reached for the door, eager to get inside the captain's quarters before she was spotted, the whole time struggling to recall the right spell words so she wouldn't have to get the book out of her bag, but to her surprise, as soon as she pushed, the heavy wooden door groaned open.

Libby slipped inside the gloom and closed the door behind her. She couldn't see more than a few inches in front of her, but the scent of stale smoke, tobacco and something sickly sweet and sour hit her at once.

With a thudding heart, Libby lowered her backpack to the floor and dug around for her flashlight. But Ginny and Esmerelda must have taken it upon themselves to pack half of the *Liberté* in her bag, because she pulled out a screwdriver followed by a packet of tissues, her new slingshot Uncle Frank had made for her a few months ago, a pocket knife, a handful of her purple berries, her spell book, then a fork and spoon. Why on earth she should need a fork and spoon in this scenario was beyond her, and her vexation grew as she fumbled about in her bag, her pulse raging in her ears, knowing every second wasted created a greater likelihood of being caught.

Suddenly, she noticed a pale, blue glow emanating from the center of her t-shirt.

Of course!

She yanked the chain around her neck until the moonstone slipped out. Pale blue light spilled eerily into the darkness as she peered about the cabin.

She could see now that unlit candles were everywhere, with mountains of old wax dripping down bottles like stalactites, and

Chapter 11

wide spools of thick paper that Libby presumed must be navigational charts were stacked by a wooden desk.

She stuffed her items back into the backpack and then slipped the straps over her shoulders as she walked around the room, the whole time searching for any sign of a radio, but instead, all she saw were maps, candles, books, bottles, a few small chests and thick, wooden furniture. As she approached the bed, she realized that the odd, stinky smell she'd first noticed was coming from a huge porcelain cup lying on the floor. She yanked her t-shirt over her nose and tried not to gag, because even if the horrible smell hadn't given it away, she'd seen enough old movies to know that the cup before her must be an un-emptied chamber pot.

The pounding in her ears suddenly sank into her stomach, followed by a queasy, panicky feeling as she continued searching the cabin. The *Liberté* had all kinds of circuitry and outlets and appliances, you name it, not to mention a functioning restroom. But *this* ship ... well, there wasn't a single modern feature to be seen; no plugs, no plumbing ....

Definitely no radio.

She did spot a large, leather-bound book open on the captain's desk, so she went to it, thinking that if it was the captain's log, then it might at least provide some useful information.

Libby bent over the book and peered at the open page. Spidery script floated over the paper, forming sentences with strangely spelled words. But other than catching the word *"Liberté"* three-quarters down the right page, she didn't get far into reading the rest of it because the light from her moonstone flashed over the top corner, and what it revealed made her blood run cold.

Libby forgot all about the nasty smell, about that panicky

feeling in her gut, about everything except four numbers etched in the corner of that page.

"Holy crud," whispered Libby, still not quite believing what she saw, and with each breath, her dread flooded back. She slapped her face, then rubbed her palms over stinging cheeks, blinking furiously the whole time before daring to look again. The numbers were still there, neatly scrawled directly after the entry "August 17."

But it wasn't the day or the month that was hard to accept; it was the *year*.

Because directly after August 17 came these four digits:

1871

Chapter 12

The Disappearance

"Oh-oh-oh!" Libby gasped, her voice trembling with her panic. "We're in *1871!* Uncle Frank's machine has teleported us to the *South Pacific* in *1871!*"

Her ears pounded harder and harder, *boom-boom-boom*, and her fingers gripped the leather-bound book as she stared hard at those numbers. As impossible as it seemed, she couldn't deny that all the facts added up: the strange clothes, the odd manners, the sailors' astonishment at all of Uncle Frank's inventions, the definite lack of modern appliances on the *Leonora* ... and no radio.

Is that what Uncle Frank had been trying to tell her right before he fell asleep? Had he figured it out, too? What had he said ... something about the machine downstairs and how their communication equipment and anything run on satellites ....

Of course nothing that runs on satellites will work, Libby realized sickeningly, because although she couldn't say *when* satellites were invented, she knew with absolute certainty that they didn't exist in 1871.

Libby's heart raced faster and faster as the awful truth sank in.

And what about that story Uncle Frank had told them, right before they'd been attacked by the rock-throwing women? About that strange wizard named Sheng who'd visited Uncle Frank in Burma, claiming to know the secrets to time-space travel, secrets Uncle Frank confessed to be more or less obsessed with?

Boom-boom-boom, persisted Libby's heart. She continued to stare at those four, incredible digits etched across the top right page, her mind racing as much as her pulse, grabbing at facts like spilled coins from a purse, desperate to put things in order again. Without thinking, she gripped the moonstone amulet in her fist as if it could stop the racing of her heart, and shafts of pale blue light shot between her fingers. She looked at the beams of light, momentarily dazed, and then remembered that the whole story about Sheng and Uncle Frank's machine was tied to the moonstone ....

Libby squeezed her eyes shut to concentrate, trying to recall all that Uncle Frank had told her. But even without his story, she already knew the amulet in her hand held magical powers. Aside from the fact that it was currently glowing, she'd witnessed the magic of the other two when Zelna and the stones had exploded into dazzling blue light.

Even eight months after that awful night, Libby had never been able to shake the feeling that, despite what she'd seen in the cave, Zelna wasn't completely gone. But the one thing she *was*

Chapter 12

certain of was that, when the moonstone's powers were combined with her own freakish abilities, all kinds of bizarre things were bound to happen.

The realization made the booming in Libby's ears stop. The fragmented thoughts that she'd been trying so hard to grasp suddenly came together in her mind, with three facts in particular racing to the forefront:

One, that today was—or at *some* point had been—her birthday, an event that was much more significant than your average eleven-year-old's birthday. Because for Libby, that meant her own unique binary star system—or whatever Sabine had called it—was now aligned, making Libby's magic more powerful.

Two, if Libby's magic was more powerful, that meant her presence would be more visible to others in the Coven of Hessen. This also meant that, if she was right and Zelna really *was* still around in some shape or form, perhaps she'd somehow tapped into Libby's power.

Finally, there was Fact Number Three, the one that tied all of this together: It was Libby's special day, when her powers reached its peak; she'd been near the moonstone necklace and the controls of Uncle Frank's new invention that, whether he realized it or not, contained the necessary components to fulfill Sheng's theories of time-space travel; and then that sudden storm exploded just when Uncle Frank activated his machine with Libby nearby ....

Boom, boom, boom, echoed Libby's heart, Libby's head, down into every part of her being. Because here was Fact Number Three:

It was her own freaky powers that had sabotaged Uncle Frank's machine, activated whatever unlocked secret it was that must have opened some sort of "wormhole" as Uncle Frank had called it ... and transported them to 1871.

The room swam before her eyes.

1871. The thought rang in her head, this time clear as day. *We're in 1871 ... with no way to reach anyone ... and no machine to bring us back!*

A sob shuddered out of Libby as she turned to the door. And then, before she even knew what she was doing, she was running through it, her legs pumping wildly beneath her as if, somehow, she could outrun this awful reality.

She ran past the ladder and dashed across the wooden deck with no care about waking the sleeping sailor or anyone else for that matter, because the only thought she had was that she needed to get Ginny, get back on that rowboat and get out of there before she did anything terrible.

She didn't know a thing about the actual science of time travel, but she'd read enough science fiction books to know that anything you do in the past can irrevocably change the future, anything at all. She could slip on a pebble and somehow, that silly little act could spawn a chain of events that could change the future ... maybe even make it cease to exist. And while she wasn't *in* the future, her parents still were, and *that* thought flooded out everything else.

Her brain raced through everything that had occurred over the evening, questions swirling like a hurricane. What if it was too late? What if the dinner with the sailors had already done some kind of irrevocable harm? What if her parents were already affected somehow? What if she'd already hurt them?

Libby ran to the cargo netting, desperate to reach the rowboat. The night could not get any worse, of that she was certain, and the only hope she had left was getting back to Uncle Frank

Chapter 12

before she did anything else stupid. If she could just do that, perhaps he would know what to do; maybe he could use the power of the moonstone necklace after all. Maybe if the stone worked with Libby's own powers to activate the time machine, maybe it could repair it, too ....

Libby reached the cargo net and flung her leg over the side. She leaned on the rail, sliding her torso over when suddenly, she froze in mid-motion. Her eyes popped wide in alarm, the pounding in her head feeling like it might explode out of her ears, because suddenly she realized she had been very, very wrong.

The night *could* get worse.

And it just had.

A gasp pushed out of her as she stared at the sea below. The rowboat still bobbed in the water, directly under her current position, just as she'd last seen it. The cargo net hung slimy and limp, just as she'd last left it. In fact, everything was exactly as it had been when she'd tiptoed over the deck not fifteen minutes ago. Everything but this:

Ginny was not there.

Chapter 13

Gentlemen of Fortune

"Oh, no," Libby breathed as she stared at the empty boat below. "No, no, no!"

She tore her gaze from the boat to the water around, searching for any indication of Ginny's whereabouts. A thousand possibilities exploded in her mind. Ginny couldn't just *disappear!* Had she fallen into the water and somehow been sucked under the ship or something?

Libby didn't have the chance to dive into the water and find out. The unmistakable stench of onions and garlic wafted under her nose, freezing her frantic thoughts.

Libby spun around.

A huge, hairy sailor towered above her—a different one from the sailor sleeping in the pile of ropes—and for three

Chapter 13

stunned seconds, all Libby could think of was how such an enormous person could sneak up on her so quietly.

"That's enough skulking about, girlie," came his gruff voice from far above, "and I'll thank you to hand over that pretty little trinket."

Before she could even make sense of what was happening, she felt the moonstone necklace plucked from her neck and, in the next instant, she was lifted like a sack of potatoes and slung over a hairy shoulder. Her stomach hit hard against the sailor, knocking the breath out of her.

"Where's my friend?" Libby wheezed, barely able to form the words. "What have you done with her?"

But the hairy man only snorted in reply and continued walking over the deck, the motion bouncing Libby's head up and down so that the boat and the man and everything else blurred in her vision. Even so, she knew from the voices around that there were several men on deck now—maybe as many as five or six—speaking a mix of English, French and something that sounded similar to what the rock-throwing women had spoken.

She could also tell from the splashes of light blinding her eyes that they carried lanterns. Where everyone had been when she'd first sneaked aboard was beyond her, but she had the impression from the pungent smell of grog that perhaps they'd been below deck having dinner.

Libby held her breath, desperately trying to avoid the terrible combination of body odor and nasty grog, but between the smell and her head-bobbing and the random glare of lantern lights, she was too overwhelmed to effectively fight back, and anyway, she considered miserably, what was the use? Even if she could get free, where would she go? She wasn't about to leave the *Leonora* without finding Ginny first, so she'd just have to go along with things until she could decide what to do ….

The hairy man shouted something to a sailor who had come on deck; Libby heard the creak of hinges from somewhere below her—perhaps some sort of trap door, she considered vaguely—and in the next moment, she knew without a doubt that it was a trap door because she was dropped through it.

The sensation of falling is almost always a disconcerting feeling, but when one doesn't know where one is falling *to,* it is much, much worse. Screams pierced the air as Libby fell through the hole in the deck, her hair whipping about her face, and she didn't realize at first that it was her own voice she heard, and when she finally *did* realize it, the whole thing was doubly strange because then, she couldn't stop herself. Although the fall probably only lasted a second or two, it felt like one endless, terrifying stretch of time. When Libby finally landed, the impact once again knocked the breath from her lungs, and it took another second or two to realize she had actually been caught by another equally stinky—but slightly less hairy—sailor.

Libby gasped in a mouthful of stale air, blinking into the gloom. She was somewhere in the bowels of the ship—that much was obvious—but all she could make out were the shadowy forms of what she supposed were wooden barrels piled high around her, and when she turned to look up at the face of the person currently holding her, all she could see was the glitter of his eyes.

Libby shuddered and turned away, the momentary terror of free-falling into a dark abyss rapidly replaced by the creepy sensation of being held like a baby by a South Seas sailor from the late 1800s.

The man started to walk, his footsteps thumping against the

Chapter 13

floor planks as he carried her, the sound echoing oddly in the damp, mildewy air.

Libby squeezed her eyes shut—a very unnerving thing to do when being transported by a stinky stranger, but she was desperate to adjust to the darkness so she could better make out her surroundings. When she opened her eyes again, she found that they were now in a wider storage area of the ship—presumably what Esmerelda had called the hold—and a single candle burned on a metal plate at the far end, casting enough light for her to make out some of the hold's features.

And that's when all of the strange, befuddling and downright bizarre things that had happened since she'd first woken up that day (even though technically, "that day" had begun nearly 150 years in the future), finally came full circle.

Libby's arms rippled with goose bumps as she stared in horror around the dimly lit space, because what she saw was exactly what Esmerelda had described, and even though Libby had known before sneaking onto the *Leonora* that there were likely people held captive on board, it was another thing altogether to actually *see* those people.

Also, while discovering that she had been transported back in time, finding Ginny missing and being kidnapped by garlic-scented sailors, the fact that there may be captives on the ship had momentarily escaped Libby's thoughts. But there was no denying what she saw now.

Along one side of the hold, boys and men sat chained together, their ankles and wrists bound by wide, metal clasps, while the clasps about their wrists, in turn, were connected to a central chain that ran along the length of the hold. Libby looked into their faces as she was carried past.

While some of the younger boys were sleeping, most of

the prisoners seemed awake but kept their gaze directed toward the ground—some had faces so badly beaten that they couldn't have opened their eyes if they'd wanted to, and only one or two raised their heads enough to return her gaze. All were as silent as the grave, with nothing but the *clomp-clomp-clomp* of the sailor's tread to be heard.

The goose bumps on Libby's arms turned into goose boulders as she recognized a few of the faces—they were just as she remembered seeing them when she'd stared at the rock-throwing women from the safety of the *Liberté*'s cabin!

She couldn't believe it; it was strange enough to discover Esmerelda's heat-sensor theory that people were held captive in the ship's cargo was spot-on, but stranger still to realize that, in a way, she'd actually *met* these people before; that she'd even felt the terror of their loved ones—women and girls who where these captives' mothers, wives, daughters, sisters ….

Libby gaped at the captives, overwhelmed by a sudden resurgence of emotions—emotions that came straight from the rock-throwing women. She was sure of that now and, more than that, she saw the images in their minds again; the faces from the women's memories flashing between the faces Libby now saw in the flesh.

And she could see more than that, too. She had no idea how or why this was happening, but as she looked into the downcast faces of the captives before her, she caught glimpses of scenes leading up to their imprisonment.

It was so strange; it was if she were watching a movie in her mind, only instead of the whole movie, she only saw little pieces of scenes that began and ended at random times:

She saw the *Leonora* anchoring just outside the ring of coral reefs that surrounded the island; she saw the sailors emptying

Chapter 13

into rowboats, bringing beads and cloth and metal trinkets to that remote, cupcake-like land, things they knew would delight the people who dwelled there.

She saw a feast and dancing—everyone laughing and having a wonderful time—and then, as the women and girls began performing a traditional dance for their guests, a mass of confusion as unsuspecting men and boys were suddenly corralled together at gunpoint. She heard a gunshot from somewhere out of sight, then women screaming and clawing at the sailors, but it was too late because all the islanders were surrounded by guns and completely unprepared to defend themselves.

She saw Captain Hayes directing the sailors as they forced the men and boys into rowboats, then turning to the terrified women with that wide, bright smile of his, as if he were doing them some sort of favor by kidnapping their brothers, fathers, husbands and sons.

It was horrible. And though she did not see this particular scene, she was certain that some of the people from that island must have perished at gunpoint. What she *did* see was so vivid in her mind that Libby forgot she was now a captive on that same ship; instead, it felt as if she were actually *there* on the island, watching it all with as much helplessness as the women, children and men, feeling their fury and their fear.

"Belay that nonsense, girlie," came a gruff voice; it sounded English. "It's not like we be selling ye, too!"

Libby started, immediately brought back to the present, suddenly realizing that tears ran down her cheeks. She looked up at the sailor who was carrying her, the one who'd just spoken, and could see enough now to determine he had blue eyes, longish black hair, a wide, ruddy face, and a crooked nose that she wanted very much to make even more crooked. It was clear from his expression that he found her distress ridiculous.

Well, she didn't care *what* he thought because she hated him. She hated all of these horrible sailors. How could anyone do something so awful? The scenes she'd just witnessed made her blood boil with rage.

"You are a murderer ... a kidnapper ... and a thief!" Libby sputtered, shaking with fury. But as she spoke those words, it struck her that there was one word in particular that perfectly described this sailor—that described all of the sailors on the *Leonora*—and it wasn't a word she'd ever expected to use on a living person:

"You ... you're a *pirate!*"

"I'm a gentleman o' fortune," corrected the sailor, sneering at her as he lowered her to the floor.

Libby was so angry she couldn't even see straight. She forgot all about her plan to go along with things until she found Ginny. Instead, as soon as she was freed from the man's grip, her hand formed a fist and then, before she'd really thought the whole thing through, that fist landed smack in the center of his crooked nose.

A startled curse pierced the air, but Libby was too stunned to decipher what it might mean. She'd never actually punched a person before, much less a pirate, and the act of following it through was a lot different than she'd imagined.

"Ow," she said, shaking her hand.

"Little wretch!" roared the sailor.

"Holy Macaroni!" whimpered another voice, and it wasn't until that moment that Libby saw Ginny huddled in a corner, not five feet away.

Chapter 14

The Boy in the Shadows

"Ginny!" Libby gasped in relief. She was just about to kick the sailor and grab Ginny to make a run for it when Ginny broke into sobs.

"I'm tied to this ... pole," she wailed, her messy, loose hair now missing its ponytail holder altogether, "and I was so scared—"

"Did they hurt you?"

"Shut your tator-trap!" roared the sailor, pushing Libby to the ground. "You're more trouble than a full-grown woman, and that's saying somethin'!"

As the sailor continued to hiss more nasty things at Libby while tugging her arms behind her back, she realized with increasing dismay that punching a pirate in the nose probably hadn't been the smartest strategy.

The sound of clinking chains drowned out the sailor's cursing and, seconds later, metal clasps closed around Libby's wrists, then two more clasps snapped around her ankles, followed by the click of keys into locks.

The sailor was still cursing as he stood up. Slipping the ring of keys dangling from a chain around his neck back under his shirt, he stomped out of the galley while shouting "Best learn yer manners!" followed by another string of words Libby had never heard before.

Libby glared after the man, wishing more than ever that she could send lightning bolts from her eyes, or electric eels, or a hundred canoes filled with furious, rock-throwing women.

"What was he saying?" sniveled Ginny.

"No idea," Libby muttered through clenched teeth, "but I don't think any of it was a compliment."

Ginny suddenly stopped crying as she shook her head for a moment in silence. Then, in a voice that almost sounded amused, she exclaimed:

"You just punched that guy in the nose and called him a *pirate!*"

"That's because he is one," replied Libby uneasily; she wasn't sure what to make of Ginny's sudden change in emotion, not to mention the fact that her own current sitting position was extremely uncomfortable. While Ginny only had a rope tied around her torso and arms that cinched her to a wide, wooden post, Libby was bound in chains and had her arms twisted behind her back, which was made all the more uncomfortable by her backpack, forcing her to sit at an awkward angle.

"Don't be silly," said Ginny. "I've thought about it, and

Chapter 14

we're obviously in some kind of weird re-enactment. I was panicking at first, but now that you're here, I'm feeling much better; we just need to stay logical and stick to the facts. Isn't that what you always say whenever we're trying to figure something out?"

"I guess I do. So I should tell you that—"

"And what I know for a *fact*," continued Ginny, ignoring Libby, "is that ruffly-shirt pirates in old, wooden ships don't exist anymore; the only pirates around today are people who make illegal copies of movies ... or those guys in the news who take over cargo ships with powerboats."

"They sure exist in the 1800s ...."

"I bet all of this is fake," persisted Ginny as she looked around. "Maybe we're secretly being filmed for a show or something."

Libby realized her friend had that peculiar tone to her voice—the same tone she always got in especially distressful situations ... right before she totally lost it.

"You know," Ginny rambled on, "one of those *Caught on Camera* things. I bet all these guys are just actors, pretending to be prisoners; I bet all that stuff about you seeing their faces before was just some malfunctioning witch-glitch!"

"I wish you were right," replied Libby, shifting uncomfortably, "but I might as well break it to you straight."

"What's that?"

Libby thought for a moment. Well, that was the problem, wasn't it? How could anyone *break it to her straight* and sound remotely sane?

Libby took a deep breath. It was now or never.

"You know how, after Uncle Frank's machine malfunctioned and you said everything on deck got all weird and stretchy-like?"

she began, but Ginny stared back at her as if she'd just recited a deeply sentimental poem in Elvin tongue.

"And then," Libby continued, "remember how there were no lights to be seen anywhere, and how our radio, cell phones and GPS wouldn't work?"

"That only happened earlier today, Libby. I'm not *that* forgetful!"

"And then, Uncle Frank told us about his invention downstairs, about that wizard guy Sheng who talked to him years ago about theories on space-time travel …."

"And how Uncle Frank realized that his machine had teleported us to the South Pacific," Ginny interrupted. "Yes, I remember all that. What's your point?"

"Getting there," said Libby. She shifted again; her shoulders were already aching like crazy. She couldn't imagine how the other prisoners were able to sit this way for hours—days, even.

"Then of course we saw those women in the canoes who were dressed funny, like they were out of some history book," continued Libby, "and the only weapon they had was that really old gun … and then remember how they were totally freaked out when Uncle Frank revved up the diesel engine, as if they'd never heard an engine before?"

Ginny's brows drew together in irritation.

"Of *course* I remember! It just happened today! Tell me something I *don't* know!"

"Okay," said Libby. "We're in 1871."

"What?"

"August 17, 1871, to be more exact. I saw the date written in the captain's log!"

"We … *what?*"

"I think I accidentally did something to Uncle Frank's

Chapter 14

machine," Libby continued, and now that she'd said it out loud, the idea seemed a lot less difficult to explain. "I remember feeling really strange as soon as I got on the *Liberté* this morning—as soon as I left my mom's side, in fact—and then I remember a flash of lightning, just as Uncle Frank turned on his machine ... and then, it felt as if something was taking over me, I don't know, but the next thing I remember is everything going black!"

"I don't see how that has anything to do with 1871," replied Ginny with a sniff. "And anyway, like I said, we're in some sort of re-enactment, so of course the captain's log would say 1871. Even silly TV shows should at least *try* to be historically accurate!"

Libby shook her head. "You don't understand! Something's *happening* to me; remember how Sabine said I've got some kind of binary star system or something that lines up on my birthday, making my powers stronger? Well, today is my birthday! I'm not quite putting it all together just yet, but something is definitely happening to me. And that *something,* I'm pretty sure, sabotaged Uncle Frank's machine and transported us to the South Pacific in 1871!"

She was speaking very quickly now, the words tumbling out as rapidly as her thoughts created them.

"Remember Uncle Frank mentioned theories on wormholes? You *saw* it, Ginny! You said it looked just like *The Scream* painting, remember? That's because we didn't just teleport to the South Pacific; we went through a wormhole and traveled through *time!*"

There was a long pause.

"I think you've got a concussion after all," Ginny said after another moment. "Or maybe it's your blood sugar. Have you been tested for diabetes?"

Libby rolled her head back in frustration, not knowing what else she could say to convince Ginny of the truth, but just as her head tilted up, her eyes met something else instead of the ship's rafters. And what she saw was a boy who stood in the unlit space behind her, watching her in amazement. Libby blinked up at him, equally surprised, but in the next moment, he stepped from the shadows and stood in full view before them.

"I do not know of these other things she speaks of," the boy said, looking at Ginny, and his voice was low and musical, his accent like that of a British stage actor. "But I can confirm today's date with complete certainty. It is indeed the seventeenth day of August, in the year of our Lord 1871. And now, I would like to enquire ... what day did you *think* it was?"

Chapter 15

Blackbirding

Libby wasn't sure what Ginny was more stunned by: the fact that a boy was standing before them speaking perfect, non-pirate English or the fact that he'd confirmed they were in 1871.

The boy turned to Libby and asked, "Is your friend of sound mind? Her behavior seems … peculiar."

"She's fine. Just had a bit of a shock," answered Libby, still watching an uncharacteristically speechless Ginny. Then, slowly, she turned back to the boy, for the first time taking in his appearance.

He was a few inches taller than her, but she supposed he might be her age—maybe a couple years older at most—although it was always hard to tell with boys. He had the brightest brown eyes she'd ever seen lined with long, dark lashes. His wavy hair was dark, too, and his light brown skin had a warm glow that immediately reminded her of sunlight, even though she knew that didn't make any sense. He was barefoot, but a pair of leather shoes were strung together through buttonholes with a piece of twine and hung over his left shoulder.

"They are not comfortable," he said, smiling sheepishly as he glanced from his feet back to Libby, "so I take them off when no one is looking."

Libby didn't understand why exactly, but her face flushed with heat, and when she looked back at him, she suddenly felt nervous.

"What's your Libby?" she blurted before she realized what she'd just said. "I mean, I'm name. I mean, what's your name? I'm Libby … and this is my best friend, Ginny. Or, er, sister—"

"It's complicated," interrupted Ginny, recovering enough to raise her eyebrows in Libby's direction. "And I'm of perfectly sound mind, thank you very much."

"I am Kaivai, but you may call me Kai as I have learned that is easier for the Western tongue," the boy said, glancing curiously between Ginny and Libby. "I have been on this ship for two hundred days. Before then, I was on another."

"But you're …," Libby paused, unsure of how to ask the question without sounding like an idiot, "… not a pirate?"

"A pirate?"

"You know, a bad guy. Did you have anything to do with capturing these people?"

"Certainly not!" retorted Kai. "How do you think I came aboard this ship? I, too, fell victim to the schemes of that madman!"

Libby was just about to apologize when Ginny laughed a sharp, bark-like laugh.

"Oh, you're good. You've got the righteous anger down and

Chapter 15

everything—totally believable! I always wondered: how much do they pay for this kind of work? And how do you get into it?"

Kai's eyes flashed.

"She's just joking," Libby quickly said, glaring at Ginny.

"I am not! I'm getting really tired of being tied to this pole and, what's more, I don't think it's fair I'm acting *for free* while this guy is obviously paid staff or something!"

"Ginny!"

"I do not appreciate the light manner in which you speak of my misfortune!" rejoined Kai. "I may be the cabin boy, but that is certainly not by choice. And as for *pay*," he added, casting a hard glance Ginny's way, "I suppose I receive the benefit of my life ... for now. In return, I must witness atrocities inflicted upon my neighbors."

"Do they teach you to speak like that?" said Ginny with a sniff. "Or are you just making it up as you go along?"

"Ginny!"

"I shall tolerate no more of this foolishness," the boy declared, turning abruptly and stalking away. But just as he reached the passage leading from the storage room, he stopped. With an annoyed sigh, he turned around.

"But I also can not hold you responsible for your friend's calloused words," he said, addressing Libby. "And I know from experience the terror you must be feeling. At least you can take comfort in the knowledge you will not share the same fate as these unfortunate souls."

Libby turned her head to follow his gesture, but from where she currently sat bound and chained, she couldn't see anything of the other prisoners except the side of one man's face. A low groan came from his direction.

"Can't you unlock their ... er, shackles or something?" she

asked, feeling a little strange to be using a word like *shackles* in normal conversion. "I've only had these on for a few minutes and they're killing me. I can't imagine …."

"I am certain these shackles would not prove fatal to you," replied Kai solemnly, "but in any case, the only man here with a key is the one you bludgeoned. He is indeed cruel. It is senseless to keep these men bound in this way. They are so beaten and dispirited that they do not dare move, especially after what happened the last time they attempted escape At least they are not deprived of food," he added darkly. "Hayes wants his cargo strong when we reach our destination."

"What destination?" asked Libby, but Kai shook his head as he watched her, his gaze alert and thoughtful.

"You must answer my question first. You are strange people to come aboard this ship—I saw the manner in which you arrived, and I mean to understand your behavior. Why do you claim that your friend does not mean what she says? Surely she is aware of her own words. And beyond that, she can see for herself the misfortune around her."

Libby blinked, trying to remember what she and Ginny had been discussing; there were so many things happening at once that it was hard to keep track. She glanced uneasily at her friend, who only glared back at her.

"Well, I'm not sure how to explain it," Libby replied slowly, "but I think she thinks this is some sort of show."

"A show?"

"Yeah … like a game—a play, I guess. There are shows like this where we, er, come from, and she thinks …."

"Where *do* you come from?" interrupted Kai, coming closer.

Libby chewed her bottom lip, suddenly feeling extremely

Chapter 15

ill-equipped to discuss her origins with an exceptionally good-looking cabin boy from the nineteenth century.

"Let's say we are from the States—I mean the United States of America," she clarified, remembering that someone from 1871 might not know what the *States* was. "Does that help?"

Kai stopped beside a mildewed barrel and scowled down at her. "Captain Hayes is from the United States of America."

"Er, unfortunately, yes," agreed Libby. "And on behalf of my country, I'd like to formally apologize for having such a horrible citizen …." She glanced at Ginny for support, but her friend just pursed her lips.

"Whatever," Ginny eventually said. "If this *isn't* actually a show, then what's your explanation for being on this ship? I think I deserve to know that—especially if I have to stay tied to this stinky pole!"

Kai considered them both with a solemn expression.

"Very well, I will tell you," he said. He lowered himself to the floor, then crossed his legs, resting his hands on his knees.

"I am from a small island near another called Vava'u; some would claim we are now part of an island kingdom called Tonga, but many of us are still in disagreement about that—we are in these waters now. In any case, I learned English from the missionaries who arrived years ago. It is because of my English that I am now a cabin boy instead of a slave at a sugar cane plantation in Fiji or Tahiti. That is where these poor fellows are headed," Kai added, gesturing sadly to where the prisoners sat.

"It is a fate common amongst our people now: Westerners arrive on our islands by trickery, pretending good will and presenting gifts we have never before seen. And then, when we least expect it …."

"They round you up with guns and force you onto their

ships," interrupted Libby in a whisper. "That's why the women were so angry earlier," she said, turning her head toward Ginny. "It was bad enough that their men had been taken by *this* ship, but when we showed up on the *Liberté*, they thought we were coming for them! They thought we were pirates, too!"

A strange expression crossed Kai's face. "I have seen your ship in the distance," he said. "It does indeed look like it could be another blackbirding vessel."

Libby shook her head. "Sorry, uh … *blackbirding?*"

"It is a term used for those who steal humans and sell them as slaves. And often, in so doing, kill others who stand in their way." Kai's brow was knit in anger. "Captain Hayes is famous for this craft. He has sailed for years, switching between ships and home countries, marrying new wives for their wealth after his previous ones have mysteriously met untimely deaths, stealing humans and selling them as slaves as easily as others change their shirts. And yet, he never fails to charm wherever he goes. He is quite witty and gallant when he wants to be. No one ever suspects the evil lurking beneath."

"Well, *we* did," said Libby. "That guy gave me the creeps before I ever knew who he was!"

"And yet, I venture that even you did not suspect him capable of what you have witnessed here."

Libby was still thinking that over when a rough voice from beyond the passageway barked out Kai's name. Kai startled and then grabbed his shoes, swiftly slipping them back on and buttoning up the strange button holes.

"I must go," he said as he rose to his feet, and with that, he left the room.

Chapter 16

Golden Treasure

Libby stared into the blank passageway into which Kai had just disappeared.

Her head spun with all that he'd told her, much so that for the moment, she forgot her own situation wasn't much better than that of the shackled prisoners. And if it hadn't been for the strange sensation of something running over her leg, she probably would have remained that way for a long time.

But something *had* run over leg, and when she glanced down, she witnessed a brown, fury rat darting away from her ankle and into the gloom.

Libby bit back a yelp; she hated rats! Well, it was more of a terror-thing than hate, but either way, the last thing she wanted at this particular juncture was for a nasty rat to crawl over her! And worse, if Ginny found out there were rats, everyone in the hold would have to deal with delirious, earsplitting shrieking, too.

Libby pressed her back against the post, wishing desperately to break free from her chains and scramble to a safer spot. Her skin crawled as she searched the shadows, her pulse pushing so hard against her wrists and neck and temples that it felt as if it might break through, and just then, she caught another movement by the wooden barrels.

This time, she saw several furry objects clustered together by one barrel in particular, and now, she could hear their high-pitched squeaks. She held her breath, her heart thudding harder and harder as she stared at the rats, as if staring at them would somehow make them go away, and as she did this, the strangest thing happened:

Through the *boom-boom-boom* of the pounding in her ears, those high-pitched squeaks suddenly sounded almost like … *words!*

She gulped in the stale air, trying to slow her heartbeat, taking calm, deep breaths until she could hear the squeaks more clearly, certain she must be imagining things, every inch of her body strained in concentration. But then, as she listened, the hair on her arms bristled into pins; her skin and her eyes and her ears zinged with an electric sensation because, as unlikely as it might be, she knew now without a doubt that she *was* hearing words.

And as she listened, those words turned into sentences, and before Libby could think to pinch herself (which was just as well, because it is rather difficult to pinch anything when one's wrists are twisted behind one's back and shackled by ancient instruments of torture), she was hearing the most bizarre conversation.

Chapter 16

"Don't be so high and mighty about it," scolded an exceptionally high-pitched voice coming from the general direction of a barrel. "She can't help it if she smells funny."

"All of them down here smell funny," said another. "Onions! Don't they know that humans should smell like onions? Take that away, and they smell ridiculous!"

"Ridiculous?" giggled a young-sounding voice. "What's ridiculous is their fur! What use is it at all when it's so long and stringy on their heads and practically bald everywhere else!"

"And have you ever seen such enormous feet before?" added the second voice with a snicker.

Libby blinked in astonishment as the rats continued their conversation, too amazed to care that they were now making fun of her clothes. *Well, at least I have clothes*, she whispered to herself.

"What's that?" came an annoyed squeak.

Libby yanked her head back in alarm, then looked around, her gaze falling on Ginny. "You said something?" she asked.

"No," glowered Ginny, "but since you asked, I think this whole thing is crazy!"

"I think it's crazy, too!" agreed Libby, dazedly turning her face in the direction of the rats again.

"Who are you calling crazy?" squeaked the same annoyed voice. "We live here; it is rude to show up uninvited only to insult your hosts, you know!"

Libby gasped, then glanced again from the rats to where Ginny sat tied to the pole.

"What?" Ginny demanded.

"Did you hear *that?*"

"Do I hear you asking me if I can hear you asking me dumb questions? Yes. And you're also making some very strange squeaking noises that I'd appreciate if you stopped doing. Things are weird enough as it is; you could at least try to act normal for once!"

"No, I mean ...."

"Young people these days!" the annoyed rat continued to scold. "No manners! Personally, I blame it on their attention spans."

Libby gulped. "I didn't mean any offense; I—"

"Libby, stop squeaking!" snapped Ginny. "You're creeping me out!"

"Ginny, please, shush!" Libby exclaimed before she could stop herself. "I'm talking to the rat!"

Ginny's eyes bulged. "You're *what?*"

"I say," said the annoyed rat, "we do prefer the term *Rattus norvegicus.*"

Libby groaned as she hung her head, wishing she could use her hands to squeeze her pounding temples. "The ... *Rattus norvegicus*," she repeated awkwardly, glancing from the barrels on one side of her to an incredulous Ginny on the other, "is, er ... well, I can hear him. And apparently, he can hear me. I'm not squeaking, Ginny; I'm speaking their language!"

For one full minute, there was utter silence. Then Ginny said, "Get yourself together! We don't have time for this!"

Libby raised her head with a sigh, then glanced at the barrels where the rats still congregated. "Will you do something to show her I'm not crazy?" she asked them. "Because, otherwise, there's no way I can explain this one."

"I *told* you, stop squeaking!" wailed Ginny.

"And what, pray tell, do you suggest?" demanded the annoyed rat, now scampering from the barrels and stopping a few feet away from her.

Chapter 16

Libby squeezed her eyes shut, trying to block out the spinning in her head that matched the pounding in her heart.

"Maybe," she considered after another moment, "you could chew through Ginny's ropes? If you could do that, she'd have to believe me. Besides, you'd really be helping us out!"

"Chew through the ropes!" exclaimed the rat in indignation, drawing up so that he stood on his hind legs.

"We … we could offer a reward?" Libby added.

The rat snorted. "What kind of reward could you possibly offer, female-*Homo-sapiens*-child? We have more here than you could ever imagine; we live in a veritable palace!" He gestured about him with a short, furry arm.

"Indeed, the only treasures *we* are interested in are those of the edible variety. To speak plainly," he continued, "we long for new cuisine. And I do not detect anything of that kind on either of you. You are nothing but a non-onion-smelling inconvenience, so why should *we* help *you?*"

Libby's mind raced, desperate to come up with an idea. It was bad enough being insulted by a rat, but worse still to realize he actually had a point, and the returning dizziness in her head made it hard to concentrate. What *could* she possibly offer? Even if she could conjure everything they had on the *Liberté*, all that would add up to was a few items in the galley cabinet ….

Then she suddenly thought of Uncle Frank, remembering when he had a case of rats in his attic once. And what had he used to trap them?

"Of course," she whispered to herself, the realization hitting her like an electric current, because what Uncle Frank had used for his attic problem was something the *Liberté* just happened to have. She turned once more to the rat and said:

"We … we come from another land," she began slowly, still

forming the thought in her mind. "Our ship is not far from here, and on it are edible treasures you've never seen."

The rat dropped his arm and peered back at her with bright, hungry eyes. "What kind of treasures?"

"Treasures that are so delicious that they are … entombed in … er, a crystal-like substance," Libby answered, struggling to think of a way to describe a plastic jar to an nineteenth-century rodent. "And the color of this treasure is golden, the texture like silk on your tongue!" she continued, now getting the hang of things.

"Ugh! Stop squeaking!" snarled Ginny.

The rat stepped closer, leaning in as he eagerly licked his lips. "What is this delight that you speak of?"

"It is called …," Libby paused for dramatic effect, "peanut butter!"

The rat drew back, his eyes wide with wonder. "It sounds glorious!"

"Oh, it is! It is so delicious that actual *lives* have been risked just for a taste of its salty, sweet goodness …."

"Enough! I can't take it!" cried the rat, raising his paws to his face. His whiskers twitched from side to side as he muttered to himself, "A *butter* substance of *peanuts!* Salty and sweet, all in one silky bite; a treasure worth risking one's life for!" And then, before Libby could squeak out a reply, he lowered himself back to all fours and darted to where the others were waiting. From where Libby sat, she could hear them discussing her request.

"The nerve!" complained one. "There's absolutely no nutritional value at all in *chewing* a rope!"

"Well, I am getting a bit long in the tooth," said another. "A good chew is just what I need to file these down. Besides, it *is* an excellent source of fiber …."

More squeaking ensued while Libby held her breath,

Chapter 16

desperately trying to capture their conversation, but all she could pick out now was "Peanut butter!"

"Right, then," announced the annoyed rat as he turned and scampered back to Libby. He raised a paw to his mouth, then whistled sharply.

In a matter of seconds, at least twenty rats scrambled from the shadows and scurried in Ginny's direction. Libby watched with a mixture of fascination and dread, because it hadn't occurred to her until that moment that an army of ship rats chewing around Ginny's arms might not be the most welcomed thing from her best friend's perspective.

"We'll do it, but on one condition!"

"What's that?" asked Libby.

The rat raised himself so he once again stood on his hind feet, paws on his hips.

"We can chew through your friend's ropes ...," his face filled with disdain at the idea, "but we can do nothing to help *you*. Therefore, *Homo-sapiens*-child, it is *she* who must bring us this fabled, golden treasure of which you speak. Promise us that, and we shall do your bidding!"

Chapter 17

The Voice from Nowhere

"YOU PROMISED THEM WHAT?!"

Libby looked nervously from Ginny to the rats chewing through her ropes.

"I'm so sorry, Ginny, but it's our only way out. Once you're free, you can take the rowboat and get back to Uncle Frank and Sal. Tell them what's happened and ...," she glanced at the annoyed rat who had paused mid-chew and was now watching Libby very carefully, "don't forget the peanut butter!"

Ginny's eyes expanded as wide as moon pies. "You want me to do all that because of a conversation you've had with a *rat?!*"

"I don't think they like that term; could you say *Rattus* instead?"

"How can you be so sure you're even *understanding* them

Chapter 17

correctly?" Ginny wailed, her eyes darting about her in terror. "This is the worst possible scenario I could ever imagine!"

"You're doing great, Ginny. Just hang in there …."

"HANG IN THERE? I'm the one with *rats* crawling all over me!"

"*Rattus norvegicus!*" corrected the annoyed rat, plucking a bit of frayed rope from his teeth. "You may use this term for both singular and plural forms of our honorable genus! It is not that difficult!"

"She can't understand you," reminded Libby.

"Arghhhhh!" screamed Ginny.

"Look, Ginny, you can do this. These prisoners are going to end up in Tahiti or something if we don't find a way to help! I know you're having trouble with all of this, but like it or not, we are *in fact* on a … blackbirding ship," she paused at the phrase, still getting used to the term, "from 1871, and you're our only hope of getting out of here!"

"Oh-ho-no-noooo!" Ginny howled.

"They're not so bad," Libby tried to assure her. "They're really smart, actually; I think you'd like them …."

"You're talking about *rats!*"

"I say, *Rattus norvegicus!*" huffed the annoyed rat. "And we have names, you know. Mine, incidentally, is Sir Jasper."

"The least you could do is answer my question!" Ginny gasped, twitching from side to side as two rats scampered across her abdomen. She squeezed her eyes shut so tightly that her eyelashes disappeared into her cheeks. "If I'm gonna sit here surrounded by rodents, you'd better give me a convincing reason to believe they're only trying to help; that you can actually understand them!"

"Just think of it like … like the time I talked to that tree, remember?" replied Libby, doing her best to make sense of it herself. "Remember how we were lost in the woods and we couldn't find our way to Hanau? And then, I just asked that huge evergreen for directions, thinking I was going crazy or something, and the tree actually pointed us to the right way?"

"There's a huge difference between a trippy pine tree and *this!*"

"But it's the same concept," considered Libby, realizing it herself for the first time. "And the same thing that let me see the images of these prisoners that the women had in their minds, that let me feel their thoughts! I ... I've been so caught up in what I'm *supposed* to do or be, that I haven't paid attention to what I already *can* do, to what's already open to me. I haven't been *listening!* And I think I'm getting stronger, Ginny. I think maybe being away from Mom has made my own powers more prominent or something. I ...."

"We are all of us thrilled you're having a personal breakthrough," interrupted Sir Jasper dryly, "but if you could inform your friend that thrashing about like a madman isn't helping any, we would be so very grateful."

Ginny's eyes sprang open. "I heard that squeak! What is it? What did it say?"

"Um ... he said wiggling around is making it difficult for them ...."

"Seriously? Difficult for *them?*"

Libby grimaced, casting an apologetic glance her way.

"Well, then you'd better keep me talking," Ginny shuddered as another rat crawled across her lap, "because it's either that or I'm going to scream my head off!"

Libby wracked her brains, but between Ginny's wails and the chattering rats discussing the most random things as they

Chapter 17

gnawed away at the ropes, well, it was rather stressful, which made it difficult to think of anything that might qualify as a conversation piece, and the annoying dizziness behind her eyes wasn't exactly helping matters.

"Say something!"

"I can't think straight!" blurted Libby. "I'm sorry, okay? All of this is my fault and no matter how hard I try, I just make things worse!"

"What ... do you mean?" wheezed Ginny.

"I mean *this!*" she said, inclining her head. "Ever since Germany, I feel like I'm going crazy! I can't sleep like I used to; I'm always tired, I'm always ... I always feel like I'm struggling—I don't know how to explain it. And then I look at Mom and I see what's happening to her and I know it's somehow my fault, Ginny, and I don't know what to do!"

"What does your mom have to do with *this?*"

"I don't know," Libby answered helplessly. "I mean, she's growing weaker and weaker for a *reason*, and even though she'd never admit to it, I get the feeling that it's because she's protecting me ...."

"Protecting you from *what?*"

Libby threw a cautious glance Ginny's way. "Well, I know this is going to sound crazy," she answered after another moment, "but I think it might have something to do with Zelna—"

"Zelna's gone!" cut in Ginny. "You saw her exploding into little blue pieces in the cave!"

But there was something in Ginny's tone that gave Libby pause. "You said that way too quickly, Ginny. You know something. What?"

Ginny's mouth puckered up as she looked from Libby to

the rats scurrying about, but as soon as she did this, she hiccupped back another wail and squeezed her eyes shut.

"I changed my mind," she said between gasps. "We don't have to talk—oh, so, so gross! I can feel their whiskers!"

"I'm really sorry," began Libby helplessly, but Ginny cut her off with a loud moan, then said:

"Look, I believe you ... about everything; I was wrong to say what I said before—especially about Kai, okay? But you can't blame me for being skeptical! It's just that everything's been so crazy today ... or yesterday, or ... whenever our wormhole-thing happened! It's hard enough to process, you know? And now ...." Her voice broke into tearful gasps, and she hung her head so that her hair fell around her face, her shoulders trembling with a mixture of sobs and revulsion as the rats continued to chew at the ropes binding her torso. "I'm surrounded by *Rattuses*," she whimpered through her tears, "and as if that's not bad enough, if I actually get free, I'm supposed to just sneak back all alone in a rowboat in the *middle of the night*, and I...," her voice dissolved into more sobs.

Libby felt terrible; there was nothing she could do but sit there and watch Ginny cry. It was such a helpless feeling, and she knew the only thing she could offer was to try and help her best friend calm down. So she took a deep breath and then, as calmly as one can possibly be when shackled in the belly of a brig headed to a sugarcane plantation somewhere in the South Pacific, said:

"I know this is scary, but we've got to stay focused, Ginny. These prisoners need our help—*I* need your help. We've got to get you back to Uncle Frank and Sal to tell them what's really happening!"

"Yeah? Well, what about me? Who's gonna help with *that?*"

Chapter 17

blubbered Ginny. "You don't even care, do you? You don't care that we're stuck forever in a century where ... where nobody even wears deodorant! Or if I die from some kind of plague I catch from this *extremely* unhygienic process ...."

"Of course I care! You're my best friend!"

"I *used* to be your best friend."

"Done!" announced Sir Jasper. He scampered over to Libby, crossing his arms in front of him as the other rats scuttled back to the barrels, chattering excitedly. "We have completed our end of the bargain. It is now time for you to complete yours!"

"Thank you, but could you just give us a moment?" squeaked Libby, looking from Sir Jasper to Ginny. In her normal voice, she said, "What do you mean you used to be my best friend? You still are!"

Ginny stared at the chewed rope on the ground beside her, as if she still couldn't quite believe what had just happened. She turned from the rope to look over at Libby, her freckled face splotched red and streaked with tears, then blurted, "So now I'm supposed to just *leave* you here?"

Libby gulped down the knot that bobbled into her throat. She'd been so focused on getting Sir Jasper's help that she hadn't had time to think about the rest of it, and suddenly, the prospect of being left all alone in the bowels of a pirate ship felt a lot more terrifying than before, and she knew that if she said anything at this particular moment, she would be begging Ginny to stay. So she clamped her jaw tight and nodded.

"Then it's time to get some things out in the open," continued Ginny, her voice growing resolute, and when she looked back at Libby, her expression was all business.

"Because even if I *can* make it to Uncle Frank and Sal, let's be honest: we don't know if I can make it back here with them before it's too late. So if I don't see you again, I want you to know that I'm sorry, too. I mean, I know things have been hard for you since I came to live with you guys—don't even try to lie just to spare my feelings. Maybe I don't act like it, but I notice stuff ... like how your parents always expect you to let me have my way all the time, not to mention I know I'm super bossy; sometimes I even get sick of myself!"

She sniveled and pushed strings of hair away from her face. "So I'm officially apologizing while I still have the chance—"

"Ginny, there's nothing for you to apologize *about!*" Libby exclaimed, cutting Ginny off, and as soon as she said those words, she knew she really meant them. Because suddenly, she realized all that other stuff—all of those negative feelings she'd kept bottled up inside—none of it really mattered. All that mattered was that Ginny was the best friend anyone could ever have, and she'd rather have to listen to her lectures than to not have her around at all. In fact, Libby realized with a pang of regret, Ginny wouldn't be Ginny if she were any different.

"I hate emotional goodbyes," interjected Sir Jasper, who still stood beside Libby's left leg, "so I will depart while your freckled friend completes her weepy monologue. Mind you, within a reasonable time frame, we do expect delivery of this golden treasure you have so regaled us with!"

And with that, he lowered his front legs to the floor and scuttled back to the barrels.

Ginny dabbed at her eyes and wiped her face, oblivious to Sir Jasper's commentary. "The truth is, I've never had anything I've really, really wanted come true until you guys came along," she continued, losing her composed manner so that her voice trembled and her eyes watered again with tears.

"When your parents petitioned for my custody, it was too

wonderful to be real; I couldn't believe I'd finally have a family—a place where I am actually *wanted*. And I was so scared your parents would change their mind—realize they've made a terrible mistake and send me back—so I overdid it, I guess. I was just trying *not* to give them a reason to get rid of me." She glanced miserably at Libby. "But it doesn't matter now, does it? We're doomed. We're stuck in this century forever—we're never going to even *see* them again!"

Libby caught her breath at that last sentence. It hung in the air like an evil vapor, and she knew if she breathed it in, she'd lose all hope. Ginny had said the one thought she'd pushed from her mind; the one thing she couldn't bear to face. Because despite all the confusing, crazy things that had happened since she woke up on her birthday several time zones and nearly 150 years away, the one thing she'd been positive about was the fact that she *had* to get back to her parents; she *had* to reach her mother before it was too late ....

But how much longer was that, before it was too late? Time was already running out. The memory of earlier that morning came rushing back: how her mom had been weaker than ever, how that white stripe in her hair had increased overnight. Libby knew the only thing that would stop it from taking over completely was if she could convince her mom to stop protecting her, but how could she convince her mother of anything when she's stuck on the other side of the globe ... in another *century?*

Libby shook her head, feeling completely lost.

Since she'd stepped onto the *Liberté* all those hours ago, it was like the world had exploded into a million pieces, and now, the parts were floating back down, forming a heavy weight over her shoulders, and what that weight told her was that until this very moment ... she hadn't faced reality. She'd clung to the idea that if they could just get back to Uncle Frank, he would know what to do; he'd find a way to return them to her parents, he just had to. Who knows? Maybe with the help of the moonstone necklace he could fix that machine after all ….

Libby hung her head, feeling the helplessness slip in at that last thought.

Ginny was right.

Even if she could make it back to the *Liberté* and then return to free the prisoners, it didn't change the fact that they were locked in another century, and now, her one possession that had given her some hope—that moonstone necklace—was gone.

Libby closed her eyes, feeling that familiar wave of nausea push against them once more, growing stronger by the second, just like it had when she'd first stepped onto the *Liberté*. The nausea expanded from behind her eyes, now filling her entire forehead, and as the dizziness took over, a thought trickled through her mind, at first a whisper until it grew into something that took up all the space inside, until it was no longer a thought but a command:

You should just give up, accept your fate, the command said. *You don't have to try so hard.*

"No," Libby whispered, squeezing her eyes shut. "I can't give up. I have to keep trying."

But the command grew stronger within her, and the more she heard it in her head, the more sense it made. *Give up, and just let things happen,* it said, and with each word uttered, her nausea grew and grew.

"What's going on?" demanded Ginny, but it sounded as if her voice floated somewhere in the distance. "Libby, what are you mumbling about?"

Chapter 17

But Libby was too overcome to hear her because now, that sickening feeling rippled from Libby's head down to her stomach; her insides felt as if they were tumbling in a giant shaker. She moaned and doubled over, unaware of anything except the overwhelming sense of motion sickness that pulsed inside of her, growing and growing, powered by the terrible command that now chanted over and over in her head:

Give up, give up, give up!

It was all she could hear; all she could think. Her brain was a swirl of chaos and confusion, as if it had somehow been pushed aside and now, something else squeezed into that space. And then, in the midst of the sickening waves that drowned out her mind and took over her body, she heard Ginny's desperate, terrified voice from far, far away:

"Libby! Libby, what's happening? Don't let her take over! You've got to fight it; you've got to come back!"

Chapter 18

Falling Stars

Uncle Frank watched as the dainty, white lights overhead flickered spastically one last time, then faded to black.

The sky was a blanket of endless void; the air so thick with moisture he thought he might choke on it. But the gloom all around was nothing to what he felt inside.

He continued to stare at the dead lights above him—the same lights that had lit their feast only hours before—as if there was something in their silence that would help him understand all that had happened.

Even after Esmerelda's confession, he was still in shock. He couldn't quite believe what Libby and Ginny had done, but the four sailors who currently lay hog-tied around the mainmast proved irrefutable.

Buttercup waddled around the sailors as if he were the

Chapter 18

appointed guard, every now and then stopping to inspect with unabashed fascination the feathers that projected from random parts of their faces. He seemed especially intrigued with the single, white plume that stuck out from the center of Hamish's forehead.

Uncle Frank turned and blinked into the darkness, into that blank, airy canvass where, somewhere, a square-masted ship bobbed above the current. And if he hadn't already known the horrible truth, he'd be praying that, any minute now, he'd see a little rowboat emerging from the mist, carrying two people in the world whom he loved more than anything.

But he did know.

Esmerelda stood by the rail, still staring at the *Leonora* with her infrared eyes. Even from this distance, she could spot the peculiar glow of Libby's moonstone necklace ... only she knew from the height and movement that it now had a different owner. And when she panned her laser sight deeper into the brig, the unmistakable heat imprint of Liberty Frye glowed back at her, a dizzying swirl of color that throbbed and pulsed with energy. But there was something different about that, too. Something about it that was ... changing.

"She-is-with-the-other-captives," reported Esmerelda, fixing her eyes on the morphing, swirling colors. "And-I-believe-Ginny-is-next-to-her, though-I-can-not-determine-that-with-certainty."

"Well, I can determine *this* with certainty," cried Hamish, and as he spoke, the white feather on his forehead wobbled in the air, "you best free us before our mates come looking! We got guns on the *Leonora*—big ones and four of 'em. Just enough to sink yer ship! We—"

Before he could finish that sentence, Sal hobbled over and stuffed a rag into his mouth. Then Sal straightened and said,

"So what do you propose, Frye? I could take our dinghy and try to sneak on board, but I don't think that'll help matters as Essie here sees a lot of activity going on. Or we could move closer and demand their release in exchange for *these* unfortunate souls—"

"We won't be doing any bargaining," interrupted Uncle Frank.

"Why?"

"Because when Hamish mentioned their 'guns,' what he really meant was cannons. And as soon as we've got the girls and they've got their men, our ship will be hit with those cannons before we can even blink."

Buttercup stopped his patrol long enough to turn and give Uncle Frank a loud *honk!*

Sal frowned. "Well, that's a pessimistic approach, Frye. Hayes here seems like a reasonable fella. He's given his word that we can conduct a peaceful exchange—"

"His word is as good as my spit in this ocean!" snapped Uncle Frank in disgust. "Trust me, McCool. I know what I'm talking about!"

Sal's mouth pinched together, his forehead creased into a hundred wrinkles. Slowly, he turned to Uncle Frank with one hand on his hip while the other pointed backward at the four sailors.

"I know this is strange coming from me," he said, "but I don't think you're being fair, Frye. I don't care for these men much more than you do, but to be honest, all I see is a captain who's been tricked, hog-tied and bewitched with feathers! Now, I want those girls back safe and sound, too, but I can't blame these fellas for being put out. That niece of yours is a bit too precocious for her own good! What kind of eleven-year-old takes it upon herself to sneak aboard a foreign ship … in the middle of the night, no less? Even you must admit she's overreacted;

Chapter 18

just look at the havoc she's wreaked on these men—not to mention what she did to *us*—all because Essie reported seeing some strange heat imprints on the *Leonora!*"

"That-is-not-exactly—" began Esmerelda, but Sal cut her off.

"She started this mess," he continued, "so why you're treating these men like the first offenders is beyond me. Let's just hand 'em over, Frye, and we'll get Libby and Ginny back!"

"And tell her to get rid of my feathers!" whimpered the sailor named John, who had downy white tufts springing from his ears that Buttercup found extremely interesting. "I fail to comprehend what witchery goes on here, but I demand we be returned to our ship with our dignity restored!"

"Can't blame him for that!" concluded Sal.

"And while you're at it, get rid of this blasted goose!" added the sailor Cal, who sported two bizarrely feathered eyebrows and was now twitching his head this way and that, trying vainly to shield himself from Buttercup's inspection.

Uncle Frank raised his hands in the air and turned around. He looked at Sal, then to where the sailors lay, then back at Sal.

"Would it change your opinion," he asked in a quiet voice, "if I told you these men are actually pirates?"

"Gentlemen of fortune," whined John and Cal in unison.

"Ridiculous," harrumphed Sal.

"Honk!" said Buttercup.

"Well, I didn't want to alarm you unnecessarily, McCool, but there is an important piece of information I've been withholding; something about our location in, er … *time*, so to speak. I wasn't sure about it until our guests arrived." He nodded to the mast where the sailors lay, and just then, one of them sneezed loudly.

"But now," Uncle Frank continued, "as impossible as it may

be, I am certain that we've done a lot more than simply teleport to the South Pacific ... and I also happen to know for a *fact* that our Captain Hayes here is a pirate ... and even worse than that, really. Because Esmerelda is right: there *are* strange heat imprints in the cargo hold of his ship, and that's because Captain Bully Hayes, as everyone called him, just happens to be the most infamous blackbirding pirate in the nineteenth century! If you kept up on your nautical history, you'd know that!"

"History?" repeated Sal in a dazed voice.

"I do declare, I believe my good name has been most egregiously besmeared by men of ill intent ...," began Captain Hayes loudly, but then one of the sailors sneezed again, which was followed by an angry oath from the captain.

Sal blinked back at Uncle Frank for several seconds. Then he turned to look at the sailors, who were now bickering with each other and squirming about ridiculously because someone's feathers had gone up someone else's nose and all four of them were either sneezing or being sneezed upon.

"I-can-confirm-Uncle-Frank's-assertion," said Esmerelda, never taking her gaze off the *Leonora*. "It-never-occurred-to-me-that-we-were-in-another-century; had-I-thought-to-run-his-name-against-my-database-in-the-first-place, I-could-have-saved-us-a-lot-of-trouble."

This got Captain Hayes' attention. He stopped his cursing and lifted his head to get a clearer view of the little robot. Sal seemed equally intrigued. And it was one of the strange moments in life when two very different people from two very different backgrounds suddenly think and say the exact same thing:

"What *century* do you think we're *in?*" they both asked incredulously.

Chapter 18

Uncle Frank looked straight at Sal, his eyes somber. "My guess is that we're in the late 1800s."

Sal's mouth dropped open.

"Are you all cracked?" declared Cal between sneezes. "Of course we're in the 1800s! We're in the year of our Lord, eighteen …."

"Silence, Cal!" commanded Captain Hayes. "Who are *we* to lecture our good, fair and exceptionally knowledgeable hosts of the proper date? Of course they know best. So, my good man …," he paused to smile genially at Sal, "please do share your impression of our current year. What year do you say?"

"According-to-my-database," said Esmerelda, ignoring Captain Hayes, "we-must-be-somewhere-between-1871-and-1874. Hayes-captained-the-*Leonora*-in-the-early-1870s, but-it-wrecked-in-1874, so—"

"It *what?*" cried Captain Hayes.

"Do-not-worry, you-make-it-alive-to-the-island-of-Kosrae," replied Esmerelda.

"Thank heavens! I mean, if I *were* this person you claim," Hayes quickly added, catching himself, "I'd like to think I'd be self-sufficient enough to make it anywhere, ship or no ship!"

"But-then-you-are-arrested."

The captain's expression fell.

"But-you-build-a-boat-from-the-wreckage-of-the-*Leonora*-and-escape-to-Guam."

"Ingenious!" the captain exclaimed with unabashed admiration. "What a fascinating, resourceful fellow this man is! And then?"

"You-continue-your-despicable-ways. In 1875, you-help-convicts-escape-from-prison-in-exchange-for-pay, then-you-are-arrested-again, you-escape-again, in 1876 you-trick-a-man-to-purchase-a-ship-for-you-and-run-off-with-his—"

"I think that's enough, Esmerelda," cut in Uncle Frank, throwing a disgusted glance Captain Hayes' way. "Suffice it to say our *guest* finally gets what he deserves—although considering all the people who have suffered from his hands, perhaps not. In any case, we'll do our best to make sure those captive aboard the *Leonora* do not suffer a similar fate."

He turned back to Sal.

"The point is, McCool, that machine downstairs somehow—miraculously—did just what our old acquaintance Sheng claimed was possible: for better or for worse, we've achieved space-time travel. And now, we're in the 1870s with four blackbirding pirates on board our ship while Libby and Ginny are somewhere on *theirs*, and I have to say, even though I am terrified and would give anything to have those two back here, I've never been more proud of my grandniece! What Libby did was selfless and brave; she went over there, risking everything to help us and save innocent people whom she suspected were held captive on board! So she may be too precocious for her own good, and she *definitely* shouldn't have snuck off like that, but don't you blame her for our current situation!"

Sal blinked again.

"You still following, McCool?"

Sal swallowed hard and nodded, his light blue eyes wide with bemusement.

"Good," said Uncle Frank. "So let's figure out how to free those prisoners like Libby planned … and get our girls back."

"You-might-want-to-speed-that-up," said Esmerelda, who, during this entire time, had not moved from her station at the

Chapter 18

side of the ship. She lifted her metal arm and pointed to the sky. "Looks-like-a-storm-is-coming."

When Uncle Frank glanced up, he wasn't sure what he was seeing. Esmerelda was right: something was definitely coming their way, but he wasn't sure *what* exactly. Through the pitch black of the night sky, bolts of lightning flashed soundlessly in the darkness, leaving tails of eerie, electric blue light behind.

"That's not like any storm *I've* ever seen," said Sal.

"What sorcery is this?" wailed Cal.

Esmerelda glanced from the blue streaks above to the invisible brig beyond, searching once more for Libby's unmistakable glow.

Her gaze caught the glow of the moonstone necklace instead, only now, she could see that its glow pulsed fiercely, as if it had come alive, and stranger still, it appeared to be *moving*... or rather, jumping into the air in spastic little tugs. She could see the heat imprint of a large hand trying to push it down, but the stone grew stronger by the second, its tugs and pulls raising the whole necklace into the air, and if it hadn't been for the chain around the owner's neck, it looked like it might zip straight into the sky.

Esmerelda shook her head and continued her search for Libby, peering once more into the depths of the brig. She found the cluster of heat imprints she'd spotted before, the same ones that she now knew with absolute certainty belonged to the captives on board. She followed their lights until she met the swirling array of colors that made up Libby's heat imprint, which was more dazzling than before, and she could see what she suspected was Ginny just a few feet beyond, moving frantically around the hold.

But when she turned her attention back to the glow of Libby's light, Esmerelda cried out in shock.

"What is it?" demanded Uncle Frank.

Esmerelda blinked, then rolled her eyes backward so the tiny little bulbs were replaced once more with her normal grey irises. She turned to Uncle Frank.

"Her … heat-imprint, it-is … *growing*. Or-rather-it-looks-like-it-is-absorbing …." Esmerelda stopped and shook her head. "I-do-not-now-how-to-explain-it …."

Uncle Frank glanced helplessly from the robot to the peculiar lights in the sky above. Even though he couldn't see what was going on in that brig, the electric ribbons of blue floating above him were enough to send prickles of foreboding through his entire body.

And then the strangest thing happened.

Even as he watched, those silent, glowing ribbons changed shape, moving toward each other like slivers of metal to a magnet, and in under a minute, those slivers had formed into an enormous pulsing, swirling blue cloud.

"What in the world…?" began Uncle Frank, but just then, a clap of thunder shattered the silence of the night. It wasn't the thunder that made Uncle Frank's blood run cold, however. It was what happened after.

A terrifying howl cut through the air from the swirling blue cloud, the sound like a million shrieks of fury that electrified everything around. The wind instantly picked up, sending rigging clanging against masts, and all around, the sea churned into peaks that grew by the second.

"What is happening?" shrieked one of the sailors, and as if by way of an answer, a black wave of seawater rose out of nowhere and crashed over the side of the *Liberté*, soaking everyone on board. Buttercup squawked and waddled to the safety of the cabin, but everyone else was frozen with fear.

"Esmerelda, what do you see?" called Uncle Frank above the chaos.

Esmerelda's lenses were already switched back to infrared as she searched desperately into the howling night. When she finally spotted the activity from the brig beyond, the first thing she noticed was the white glow of the moonstone necklace.

As before, the moonstone tugged into the air, more violently than ever, only now, she could see from the heat of the hands clasping around it that the owner was no longer attempting to keep the moonstone under control; rather, those hands were fumbling to get it *off*.

In the next second, she saw a blinding streak of light as the moonstone freed itself and zipped away from the those hands, zooming through the air as if no boundaries existed, as if no walls or people or cargo stood in its way.

Esmerelda's quick sight followed the blazing trail, oblivious to everything around but that dazzling line of white light; the terrified screams of the sailors, the crashing waves, the boat rocking perilously under her feet were nothing to the dizzying energy of the moonstone.

And then it stopped.

Esmerelda blinked in astonishment at the sight before her. In less than a second, the moonstone had gone from a frenzied blur of movement to complete stillness. The familiar shape of a circle with a peculiar, hollowed-out center now hovered in utter tranquility, and the change in motion was so surprising that it took Esmerelda a moment to realize the stone was floating just above the swirling array of lights that could only be Libby.

"Esmerelda, what do you see?" demanded Uncle Frank

again, his voice barely carrying over the storm. "Can you find Libby?"

"I-am-looking," replied Esmerelda, adjusting her focus on the dizzying throb of light. But she didn't dare say more than that, not until she knew what exactly it was that she was witnessing.

She watched as the heat from Libby's body pulsed like a giant, beating heart, and with each pulse, the differently colored lights grew and grew until it seemed as if they would fill up the entire cargo hold of the brig beyond. And as Esmerelda stood there, she could now see streaks of blue light coming from *outside* the brig, shooting from the cloud in the sky and joining the pulsing, raging swirl around Libby's body, and as she watched, tiny particles of light floated out of the frenzy like magic dust, making their way to the moonstone.

Uncle Frank glanced frantically from the little robot to the night above, and even though he couldn't see what Esmerelda saw, what he did see made him numb with fright. He no longer heard the wind's furious howl or felt the lashing spray of sea; every cell in his body was focused on that strange, electric blue cloud above.

And while Esmerelda watched the frenzied activity inside the brig, Uncle Frank saw something just as incredible outside, because now, that electric blue cloud pulsed and throbbed with renewed energy until suddenly, the cloud burst apart like a million shooting blue stars, each star falling directly from the sky, zooming straight down into the brig.

Uncle Frank gripped the arm rests of his mobile unit as he watched the display in horror.

"I-have-found-her," Esmerelda answered at last.

"I know," gasped Uncle Frank, staring helplessly as the blue

Chapter 18

lights disappeared one by one, the sky rapidly dissolving back into darkness. He was so fixed upon the display before him that he didn't hear Buttercup's honking, just as the goose spread his wings and lifted into the night sky, soon becoming a white speck in the darkness. He didn't notice that the sea had suddenly calmed, or that the wind had fallen silent as before. He just stared out into the blackness where those blue lights had disappeared, and he didn't know why or how, but somehow, he *knew* ... he knew that those lights had come for Libby.

Chapter 19

The Incident

In days to come, Libby would often wonder what might have happened had Ginny not been there. Most of what followed was just a blur in her mind, but she remembered the nausea and that awful voice chanting in her head, *Give up, give up, give up!*

Then she remembered Ginny yelling at her with tears streaming down her face, begging her not to do it, telling her she was better than that; that it was Zelna that wanted such bloodshed, not Libby.

Perhaps it was the sound of Zelna's name that finally broke Libby from her trance. When she looked around, the first thing she noticed was a sailor sprinting out of the cargo hold as fast as his legs could carry him, howling some kind of gibberish about witchcraft and the evils of womankind.

Then, she realized she was no longer sitting against a post

Chapter 19

by the casks, but rather standing in the center of the cargo hold, and if that were not strange enough, she saw that the shackles that had been around her wrists and ankles were nothing but a pile of blackened dust on the floor!

Libby stared at the pile of dust, unable to understand what had just happened. When her gaze finally moved around the rest of the room, she saw that the captives remained chained and seated along the side, their faces drawn in alarm, and that Ginny stood between them and Libby, her wide, terrified eyes locked on something in Libby's right hand that was clutched to her chest.

Libby followed her stare and discovered the moonstone amulet in her fist.

Slowly, she released her grasp so that the amulet hung freely from the chain around her neck. She was bewildered enough to find the necklace returned to her, but even more bewildered to discover that somehow, the moonstone had inexplicably changed in appearance! While the indigo blue with wispy-white swirls remained the same, the *inside* of the stone had changed and now, where there had been a hollowed-out center in the shape of a four-leaf clover, the amulet was completely solid: a perfectly round, smooth stone.

Libby glanced from the amulet back to Ginny. She opened her mouth to speak, but it felt as if her throat was stuffed with cotton.

"What ... just happened?" she finally managed to ask.

Ginny blinked rapidly, her gaze moving from Libby to something on the floor, and it wasn't until that second that Libby realized the sailor whom she had punched in the nose was lying unconscious at her feet.

Shocked, Libby stepped away, but her legs felt heavy and

uncoordinated, like her brain was having trouble telling her body what to do, and she found herself moving in awkward, jerky steps, as if she were moving through water instead of air. She didn't know if it was her strange walk or something else, but Ginny shook her head furiously, her eyes still wide.

"Stay there!" she yelped, backing toward the chained prisoners. "Don't come any closer! I'm warning you! I've ... I've taken karate and I can kick the crud out of anything!"

"Ginny, it's me!" said Libby, but even the effort to speak was exhausting. She looked at the man on the ground, a shudder rattling up her spine. "Is he ... is he dead?"

"Why? So you can torture him if he's not?"

"What are you *talking* about?"

Ginny whipped her head from side to side, her eyes never leaving Libby's face. "If it's really you, then prove it!"

Libby stared back at Ginny, trying to still the million questions racing through her mind.

"Well, you've never taken karate, for one thing," she replied in exasperation, now crouching beside the man. "And anyway, who else would I be?"

"Who do you think!"

Libby lifted her hand to the man's neck, just where his pulse should be. A faint beat replied to her touch, but even so, a feeling of foreboding crept through her. She dropped her hand and stood back up, that awkward, moving-through-water feeling still making her movements difficult.

"Just try to explain what you saw, Ginny. Could you do that? I don't remember anything after the dizzy spell ...."

"Well, that's the trouble! Because I don't know *how* to explain what just happened! There are not *words* in the English language to *describe* what just happened!"

Chapter 19

"Start with the moonstone," suggested Libby, taking a deep breath. "How did this get back to me, and how did it change shape?"

Ginny wrapped her arms tight against her torso and wriggled her lips as if trying to work up the courage to even speak. Then she blurted:

"There were these weird, blue lights everywhere and it was like a thunderstorm inside the ship!"

"*Inside* the ship?"

"And that necklace just zoomed toward you through the air—out of nowhere—just as the lights swirled around you, faster and faster, until it looked like they were kind of forming over and into you—almost like you were changing shape!" Ginny kept on, her words coming out in a rush, each tumbling into the next.

"And then, out of the lights, these dusty blue particles floated toward the necklace and ... and *filled* it, you know? And then the center glowed bright blue, and I could tell that it was the particles from our two moonstones that had exploded ...."

"You think the blue dust was actually our two moonstones from Germany?" interrupted Libby, utterly baffled.

"What else could it be? I mean, just look at your necklace now! That shape in the center of your amulet is *exactly* the same as our two moonstones from before put together! Why didn't we realize that *earlier?*" Ginny gulped, glancing from the amulet to Libby before continuing, "And then, things got super-weird. The necklace was just floating beside you and you grabbed it and put it on, and when I looked at your face...."

"What, Ginny?"

Ginny stared at her friend for a moment, and when she spoke again, her voice had calmed somewhat. "Well, you just *glanced* at the chains around you and they dissolved into dust—you didn't even *say* anything! And—and then, two sailors ran in, asking what all the commotion was about, and you turned to *this* guy and you tried to, you tried to …."

"*What?* Just tell me!"

"You were going to kill him!"

Pin-pricks swept over Libby's arms, up her neck, then into her chest. For a few seconds, it felt as if everything stood still; she even forgot to breathe. She stared back at Ginny in disbelief, but the terror in her best friend's expression told her all she needed to know.

Libby groaned and sank to the floor, her head swimming with too many sensations, but the worst one of all was fear. She knew Ginny wouldn't make a thing like that up, but still, it was too terrible to fully comprehend. Because if what Ginny just said was true, then it meant ….

"I'm turning into Zelna!"

The words came out before she even knew she'd said them, the sound ringing oddly in her ears. And even though Libby had spoken in a whisper, Ginny must have heard her.

"Well," Ginny said, her voice tight with emotion, "I think it's a bit more complicated than that."

Libby could only blink in reply; she wasn't sure if she was more shocked by the horrible realization that she was somehow turning into the most evil person imaginable, or by the fact that Ginny seemed to have already known this was going to happen.

Ginny furrowed her brows, then pushed her loose hair away from her face.

"Before all the crazy lights," she resumed slowly, "when we were talking about your mom and all that, you said you thought

Chapter 19

she was protecting you; maybe even protecting you from Zelna ...."

Libby nodded, a feeling of dread trickled through her insides, settling into the pit of her stomach.

"Well, the truth is, I knew she wasn't *gone,* either," continued Ginny. "So did your parents. We all knew, Libby."

Libby felt her fingers dig into the wooden planks beneath her, as if the hard, wooden floor was the last thing left in this world that was real, that was reliable, that was what it was supposed to be.

"I heard them talking about it once," admitted Ginny. "That night in the cave, right before you fought Zelna off and shot Iorgu with your slingshot instead of me, it was ... it was really scary, Libby. I could see Zelna taking control over you. I-I thought it was too late; that we'd lost you, but somehow, you fought her off. And when I threw my moonstone toward you and there was that explosion, your mom gathered all of her strength ...."

"She was shouting words," Libby whispered, the back of her neck tingling at the memory, her sense of unease growing stronger. "Words I couldn't understand ...."

"That's what I heard your parents talking about," Ginny said. "They thought no one was around—it was after her last trip to the doctor's, you know, that time two months ago? And she was telling your dad that she didn't want to go back anymore; that there was nothing that could be done about it. They started to argue, and that's when your mom told him ...." Ginny paused and looked anxiously from Libby to the sailor who still lay unconscious on the floor.

"What, Ginny?"

"Well, you were right before, about your mom protecting

The Incident

you. She was explaining that it was a choice she'd made; it's kind of like what Sabine told you before; about how you're all intertwined or something? That one person's power impacts the other, and she'd chosen to stand between you and Zelna! Your dad was really upset and started for the door, so I took off before they saw me, but I've been thinking about that ever since."

Libby clamped her jaw and tried to swallow, but it felt as if she had a cup of whole wheat flour in her mouth.

"Man ... waking!" a voice from behind Ginny suddenly called.

Libby's head whipped up in surprise at the sound of English; it must be one of the prisoners, she realized, but she didn't have time to figure out *who* exactly, because now, a low groan came from the sailor lying on the floor.

"Quick, Ginny, we've got to do something!"

They both scrambled to the sailor's side, and in that moment, Libby saw the glint of a metal chain hanging around his neck.

"Of course! The keys!" She grabbed the chain, wiggled it over his head, and slipped the heavy chain around her neck, the ring of keys clinking against the moonstone on her chest. "Let's drag him to the shackles!"

Ginny grunted her agreement, cranking uselessly at one of the sailor's arms, as if she could use it like a boat rudder to steer him in the right direction. Libby scuttled to the sailor's feet and grabbed a leg, now pulling with all her might toward the shackles, but she still felt weak from whatever it was that had happened to her, and her feet tangled awkwardly with her ankles as sweat popped from her forehead.

"He's ... really ... heavy," puffed Ginny. "And whew—he smells *so* bad!"

Chapter 19

"Ginny, grab his other leg and help me pull this way!"

"You're the witch! Shouldn't you be able to just levitate him or something?"

Libby tried to ignore that. She glanced behind her to where the shackles lay waiting. They'd barely moved the sailor two inches, but with each second, the sailor groaned and twitched, and soon, Libby knew it would be too late ….

"Pull!" she cried between pants, but just then, from somewhere beyond, a voice blasted through the cargo hold, demanding:

"WHAT DO YOU THINK YOU ARE *DOING?*"

Chapter 20

Mutiny

A bitter taste filled Libby's mouth. Her feet felt riveted to the floor as her hands still clutched the sailor's ankle, as if her fingers had been frozen solid. A horrible, helpless feeling settled into her stomach, and she knew there was nowhere left to run, nowhere to hide.

But then, when she finally looked up, she saw it was only Kai standing in the entranceway. She nearly sobbed with relief.

Ginny dropped the sailor's leg. "Perfect timing," she announced, smoothing away the creases in her t-shirt that the sailor's boot had made. "I'll count, you guys pull. Just like before, Libby, on three. Ready?"

"Your friend," observed Kai, glancing between the sailor and Libby, "would make an excellent Quarter Master. She has a knack for having others do her bidding."

Chapter 20

"Just help!" gasped Libby, now tugging away again. "We can lock up him up and free the prisoners!"

Kai considered her for another moment, uncertainty flicking through his eyes.

"Kai," continued Libby, yanking so hard at the sailor's leg that her feet slipped from the effort, "your captain and the three guys who went with him to our ship are already tied up; they're not coming back! This is your chance to break free; you've got to help!"

Kai drew back in surprise.

"You witnessed this yourself? You saw Hayes and the rest overthrown? And if so, why did you not mention it before?"

"It's complicated," replied Ginny impatiently. "But trust us; we definitely saw them tied up ... and, er, feathered so to speak. Libby's right: this is your chance!"

Kai regarded them a moment longer, then walked over to Libby.

"You look ridiculous tugging away like that," he muttered, taking the free leg. "And I am a fool to agree to *this*. You do not know the level of punishment if we do not succeed—"

"You're right," interrupted Libby between gasps of air, "but I know what will happen if we don't even try!"

"One, two, three!" cried Ginny.

Libby could only grunt in response as she pulled and pulled, but when she glanced up again, she was amazed to discover they were close to the chain that ran through the wrist clasps of the prisoners. Beyond the last prisoner to her right, several clasps dangled unused from the chain, and as she reached backward for the pair closest to her, her eyes fell to the hands and wrists of the nearest prisoner instead.

A shudder crept through her as her gaze ran up his arms,

then stopped at his face. When his dark brown eyes met the hazel green of hers, the same thing happened as before:

A thousand pictures flashed in her mind of what the man had gone through; of what he'd seen happen to his wife, and to his three children when they'd stood up to Captain Hayes and tried to stop him. Libby sucked in a gasp.

"Hurry, child," the prisoner said in a low, raspy voice. He looked meaningfully at the sailor on the ground before them.

Libby startled at the sound, once again surprised to hear English, but she knew she didn't have time to ask questions just yet.

"Kai, twist him around so I can reach his wrists!" Libby called, yanking the clasps toward the sailor. It took a second for her to figure out the old-fashioned lock, and then several more as she fumbled with the various keys.

"The small black one," said Kai, grabbing both of the sailor's legs and spinning him around.

Libby sorted through the keys with shaking hands, now grabbing the correct key and pushing it into the keyhole.

"So you came aboard the *Leonora* with the knowledge that our captain is now captive on *your* ship…," continued Kai as the clasps snapped apart.

"Yes. We used a potion to put them to sleep and then we tied them up!" Libby tugged the clasps toward the sailor's arms. "We came over here because we were trying to find a radio to call for help …."

"A radio?"

"A … communication device; it's something we—never mind; anyway, there's no such thing here—or anywhere given the time frame! I—"

"Because *this* time frame is not what you were expecting,"

Chapter 20

interrupted Kai, watching Libby closely. "Because you are not just from another country, are you? Your clothing betrays you, as does your strange speech. I heard you and your friend conversing when you were first captured. The things you said ... curious things, using words I do not understand. But you said something about traveling through time."

Libby gulped as the shackles snapped around the sailor's wrists; for a moment she just stared at the clasps, stunned by her own success, but Kai's words floated about her, and for a reason she didn't understand, she felt guilty somehow. As if she had betrayed him without even knowing it. Or maybe not betrayed, but something else ....

"It is true, then," finished Kai in a quiet voice.

Libby nodded and glanced up at him. She didn't know what else to say.

"And the other thing I heard your friend mention; something about being a witch...."

Libby's gaze dropped from his face as she nodded again. "You don't seem all that surprised."

"Just because we are from different times," replied Kai, "does not mean human nature has changed that much. We, too, believe in the existence of such things, though those who profess to hold such powers are typically swindlers. Had I not witnessed what I have today, I would continue in that state of disbelief."

"Well, witch or not, I'm not a very good one. As you might have heard from that guy who ran screaming out of here, weird stuff is happening to me lately."

"An evil presence; a darkness that comes over you ...," suggested Kai.

Libby glanced up at him, taken aback by his understanding.

"Yeah. Exactly. Only in this case, the darkness has a name. And I ... I don't know how to control it."

Kai nodded as he continued to look at her. Then he said, "My teacher used to say it is when we are challenged that we learn who we are and what we are made of. Perhaps this is your challenge, Libby."

The skin on Libby's arms tingled, as did the hairs at the back of her neck. She looked away, feeling her face flush with heat. It was the first time Kai had ever said her name, she realized, and the sound of it did weird things to her stomach. Beyond that, was it possible what he'd just said might be true? If she survived this day, would she suddenly feel less lost? More sure of herself? Would she finally know who she was?

She didn't have much time to think about it. With the same key, she scuttled behind the prisoner who'd spoken to her and twisted the key into the lock on his cuffs.

"I can not believe I am doing this," muttered Kai, staring in dismay as the first prisoner's wrists were freed. "You may come from another time, but I am entrenched in this one. It is certain death if we do not succeed. We've little time to waste, so let us discuss your plan forthwith!"

"We don't have a plan," said Ginny, stomping up to them.

Kai blinked, then turned to Libby. "The crew knows the mayhem you caused down here; they are barricading themselves on the upper deck, stocking their weapons! I invented a lie to get away, but it will rouse suspicion if I do not return soon. This is *not* the time to be blithe!"

"Well, we do have a plan ... sort of," corrected Libby, now working on the cuffs around the next prisoner's wrists. "Our plan is to overthrow the bad guys, let these guys take this ship

Chapter 20

back to wherever it is they're from, while we get back to Uncle Frank and Sal!"

Kai's face paled, his brows drawing together. "That is not a plan. That is the *result* of a plan! Have you *any* idea what you have dragged all of us into? Or yourself, for that matter? Those men are scheming against you as we speak! They're drawing straws to determine who will be the unlucky soul to sneak down here with intentions of relieving you of your head!"

"Don't worry," said Ginny, scrambling to grab the ankle shackles that the first prisoner had just pried off. She threw the shackles at Kai and pointed meaningfully at the sailor's feet. "Your *girlfriend* here is a witch, so we've got the element of surprise on our side. Put those on the bad guy!"

Kai swallowed so hard that it looked like he'd gulped down a live tuna fish, but he caught the ankle shackles and then, with a quick glance Libby's way, turned to the waking sailor and slipped the braces around his ankles.

No key was required for these; rather, a small screw turned into place, securing the braces around the sailor's ankles. Just in time, too, because with all of the commotion around him, the sailor had recovered enough to realize what was happening.

"Unchain me this moment!" he bellowed, his eyes now wide as he thrashed about.

Libby ignored him as she worked on freeing the rest of the prisoners, her fingers moving from one lock to the next while her mind raced with questions.

Because Kai was right.

What was the plan? It was one thing to sneak off the *Liberté* to get help, but another thing altogether to overthrow a pirate ship, and even though she knew very little about the history of such things, she knew enough to know it usually ended with *someone* walking the plank. Everything was happening so fast, and what Ginny had just said about her being Kai's girlfriend made her head swim with even more questions.

"Stop it," Libby muttered under her breath, forcing her brain to concentrate on the task before her.

As the prisoners were freed from the binds around their wrists, they bent over to unscrew the clasps about their ankles. When she'd freed the last prisoner's wrists, Libby looked up and caught Kai's dark expression.

"There are heavily armed sailors on board the *Leonora*," he stated slowly. "Not even counting Pierre here."

"You will be hung like the traitor you are!" wailed Pierre, still thrashing about. "Fodder for crows; food for the fish; you shall be-omph!"

One of the prisoners had shoved what was left of his raggedy shirt into Pierre's mouth. Then he stalked over to the chewed-up rope, picked up a cord of it, and returned to tie the shirt remnant firmly in place.

"Thank you," said Ginny, nodding in approval. "One down ... how many to go?"

Kai shook his head.

"Ladies," he said, "if I may point out the obvious fact that we have officially begun the proceedings of a mutiny, I would very much like to discuss how we plan to move forward! There are ten armed men aboard this ship who won't take kindly to finding their mate bound and gagged and their prisoners set free! This is *not* merely one of those ... *shows* you spoke of earlier!"

"No problem," said Ginny with a shrug. "There's twenty-five of us!"

At this, the prisoner who had spoken earlier stepped forward. Libby hadn't realized until now how tall the man

Chapter 20

was—how tall all of them were, actually. Most of the men were at least six feet in height, and even the younger boys whom she guessed might only be nine or ten years old were as tall as she was.

"What the boy says is true," the prisoner said in his low, stilting voice. "We are brave and strong, but our hands are unevenly matched to their pistols. We have tried escape before. We have seen what they can do with their weapons."

"Well, *I've* seen what we can do with a witch," replied Ginny. "Libby, show him!"

Libby lowered her head and pushed the heels of her palms to her eyes, trying to block out her growing frustration. Ginny's over-confidence was not helping anyone sort out what to do. She knew they had to overthrow the sailors, but the question was ... how? Some of them could be lurking outside the hold at this very moment, for all she knew; she couldn't very well suggest these prisoners just show up and fight with their bare hands against swords and cannons and guns without any sort of strategy. And worse, if they were captured again, this time, Libby knew it would be all her fault ....

"If I may make a suggestion," came a high, squeaking voice.

Libby's eyes flew open at the familiar sound. She looked around, but all she could see was a tiny, pointed nose and half a set of whiskers jutting out from the nearest barrel.

"Sir Jasper!" she whispered, trying not to draw attention to herself, but the problem with that was, it's nearly impossible to speak in rat-tongue discreetly. "I'm so sorry, but your peanut butter will have to wait ...."

The rat visibly straightened as he reached out and, with his left paw, delicately smoothed a whisker.

"We do have more on our minds than simply eating," he

retorted coolly. "We are scholars, philosophers and poets—have you never heard of Shakespeare? He did not write all that by himself, you know. Sonnet Twenty-Six, for instance, my ancestor penned that—what a tortured soul he must have been! To express such poignant feeling, and then to have that scallywag William claim your hard-earned work for his own! But I digress." Sir Jasper cleared his throat as Libby blinked back at him, hardly knowing what to say.

"My suggestion, should you condescend to accept," he continued after a moment, "is that we could sniff things out, so to speak. It will only take a few minutes, and we shall be back with a report on the location of your enemies—as well as the best route to reach them—thus making a surprise attack exceedingly feasible."

"Really? You'd do that?"

"Why not? You strike me as a remarkably intelligent soul ... for a *Homo sapiens,* at least. Not many of your kind are advanced enough to speak our tongue. So I'd like to help. Besides, it would be nice to stretch our legs on a beautiful island for a while. Living on a ship can get dull, you know. We would be keen for a bit of a holiday."

Kai arched a brow Ginny's way and demanded, "What is she doing? Why the sudden squeaking?"

"Oh, this should be good," Ginny replied with a smirk. "Tell him, Libby!"

Libby glanced from Sir Jasper to Kai, then to the English-speaking captive standing across from her; he was exchanging words with the other captives in a foreign tongue, and there seemed to be a disagreement between them. She turned back to Kai. "You wanted a plan, right?"

Kai nodded, his expression once again uneasy.

"Then the plan is that the rats—er, excuse me, I mean *Rattus,*" she corrected herself, peeking over at Sir Jasper, "will find out the exact location of everyone on board. Then we can split up, attack and bring them down here to be chained up!"

Kai's eyes widened. "You *are* referring to ship rats, am I not mistaken?"

"You don't believe me," she realized out loud. Her shoulders sagged. "Of course you wouldn't. What kind of a person can speak to a *Rattus?*"

"I believe you," replied another voice.

Libby spun around and saw the tall, English-speaking captive standing before her.

"My name is Atamai and I have seen many strange things since you came aboard this ship." He turned to Kai. "She does speak the truth. The others have witnessed her powers as well—we all saw what happened when the blue storm of lights entered. I say that we follow her suggestion."

"And the other men?" asked Libby, gesturing to where the freed captives stood. "Are they in agreement?"

Atamai turned and walked over to speak to them, the sound of his foreign words mixing with those of others.

Kai shook his head as he listened to the exchange.

"I am sorry if I affronted you a moment ago," he murmured, "but I have a premonition of doom about this. I saw what happened last time the prisoners attempted escape; twelve were killed as a result, and it was not just the captain's bidding. It is why we stopped at that island you spoke of—the one where you and your crew were assaulted; Hayes needed replacements for those captives he had lost."

"What do you mean?" asked Libby, but before Kai could respond, Atamai turned toward them and said:

"It is agreed. We shall fight while we still have something to live for!"

Chapter 21

The Witching Hour

Libby's footsteps thumped dully in her ears, her pulse pounding out sound as she ran through the darkness.

The amulet around her neck had stopped glowing ever since it returned to her during what Ginny now referred to as *The Incident,* so the only light around trickled dimly from cracks in the planks above, where an occasional lamp burned away the night hours. She had no idea what time it was, but her exhausted muscles and fuzzy brain told her it had to be around midnight, maybe later.

One of the captives named Lofah ran in front of her, and behind her, Kai's bare feet padded soundlessly along the boards. Behind him, three of the younger prisoners followed.

Since Sir Jasper had returned with news of the pirates' whereabouts, the group had split into three teams: the strongest

Chapter 21

team would go first, setting up a protective defense of copra bags just outside the hatch on the deck, then carry up any items from the hold they could use as weapons: bricks and stones from the ballast, coconuts, ropes and chains ....

The second team, which included Lofah, Libby, Kai and the three captives who were still boys, would then create a diversion while the third and largest group attacked the pirate's barricade on deck.

Atamai, being the oldest of the freed prisoners, stayed behind in order to watch over Pierre and help shackle the captured pirates ... assuming the mission was successful. Ginny volunteered to stay as well.

"I mean, he shouldn't just be here all *alone;* besides, I can help lock them up," she'd said.

Libby didn't like the idea of leaving Ginny behind, but everyone agreed it was for the best. Thanks to Sir Jasper's help, they knew at least two of the pirates planned on leaving their barricade to hunt down Libby, so the farther she was from her best friend at the moment, the safer it would be for Ginny. At least Atamai was armed with a pistol they'd found on Pierre, so he could fend off anyone brave—or foolish—enough to enter the hold.

Lofah was now scrambling up a tall ladder, and as Libby followed, her heart thumped harder within her chest. Soon, they would be on the upper deck, and when that happened, she had no idea what might occur next. *Boom-boom-boom,* thrummed her chest, her ears, her head. And as her hands gripped the ladder, she felt the throbbing in her fingers as well, growing more and more frantic the closer she climbed to the top. Kai's words from earlier echoed in her mind, for a moment pushing away the drumming of her pulse, and that sense of foreboding he spoke of took hold of her as well.

A low hiss interrupted her thoughts. Libby glanced up to see Lofah's eyes flashing down, then she saw him gesture: he pointed to the open hatch above. Libby gulped down the earthquake erupting in her chest.

This was it.

In a matter of seconds, they'd be on deck, with nothing to protect them but a few stacked sacks of copra and the shadows.

She suddenly felt overwhelmingly dizzy; she clutched the ladder with all of her strength, willing herself to stay focused as she watched Lofah slip through the opening above—he made it look so easy, she mused—and in the next moment, she saw his hand reaching down to grasp hers.

For a second, she just stared at his hand. She knew he intended for her to take it, but she could climb through by herself... couldn't she?

The dizziness came back in another whoosh, and she wasn't so sure anymore. Her arms trembled as she grasped the sides of the ladder, her knees following suit. She wasn't even sure if she could stay upright as the darkness around swirled in her eyesight, and for a terrifying moment, the possibility entered her mind that she might be about to have another Incident.

Libby gritted her teeth.

"No," she whispered. "I can do this."

She grabbed Lofah's hand, his fingers wrapping around her wrist, and in the next moment she was half-climbing, half-floating through the portal.

The minute she landed on deck, belly first, she instantly felt better. Her mind cleared as she scrambled to her knees, then reached down to help Kai—a pointless gesture because he was

Chapter 21

definitely tall and strong enough to swing through the portal as well as Lofah—but to her surprise, he took it.

His grasp was warm and strong. Ridiculous. Why on earth was she thinking about his *hand* when she was about to ransack a barricade of pirates? "Stupid," she muttered, releasing his hand as soon as Kai was on deck.

"What?"

"Nothing!" She jumped to her feet and then moved toward Lofah, preparing to follow his lead as the remaining boys climbed through the opening, each turning to help the one below. Unlike Libby, who'd felt like a flailing cricket trying to half-climb, half-heave through the portal, their movements where fluid and graceful.

In the darkness, the whole thing was peculiar to see, as though it were a modern, silent dance; something her art teacher in Baluhla might pop into the classroom DVD player on a Friday and force them to watch, saying something along the lines of "This expresses the hope and despair of mankind; can't you just *feel* the *pain!*"... only "feel" would sound more like "feeaal" and pain "pay-en," and for whatever strange reason, the thought of her art teacher commenting on their pirate-sabotage almost made her giggle out loud.

"Libby!" Kai whispered, tugging her thoughts back to the present.

He gestured with his brows toward the bow of the upper deck, just before the foremast, and even in the darkness, the outline of stacked sacks and barrels could be seen, highlighted from within by the faint glow of lanterns. She recognized it at once: the pirate's barricade Sir Jasper had described.

The group moved silently away from the barricade and toward the mainmast, ducking between rigging and stepping over random piles of coiled rope. At one point, Libby almost stepped on a seabird whose brown feathers blended perfectly with the wooden deck. It scuttled out of the way just in time, but from the squawking coming from the barricade, she knew another seabird hadn't been so lucky.

She could hear voices from the barricade, too: the same strange mix of accents she'd noticed when she'd first been captured, and it seemed some of the sailors were in an argument.

"Hurry up, Hugh!" a man snarled. "We haven't all night!"

"Stop your gab and help, then," retorted another. "These spikes shan't fall on their own, you know, and we are nearing the witching hour! If Fred and Quill fail to lop off her head, this thing will get her for good! And get that blasted bird out of my way!"

Libby gulped as they crept on; she searched the deck for any sign of the others, but so far, they were nowhere to be found. The sea and sky were still, with no sound of wind to clang rigging against masts, no slosh of water against the side to disguise the sound of their footsteps.

The smell of tobacco smoke wafted through the air, and someone from the barricade let out an angry shout, followed by a string of curses.

She looked up to see Kai just inches away. He nodded, then gestured to the mainmast, where net-like ropes led from the deck to midway up the mast. Libby knew from their strategy session that these ropes were called shrouds, but it was one thing to talk about strategies and another thing altogether to act them out.

She held her breath, watching as Lofah and the three boys padded soundlessly to the shrouds and, with the agility of gymnasts, scampered up the ropes. When they reached the

Chapter 21

mainmast, they continued to climb and within what seemed less than a minute, they swung in perfect balance from different positions by the mainmast far above, commanding a bird's-eye view of the barricade below.

It wasn't until then that she noticed several figures slipping silently from the hatch, now scuttling toward the barricade, as quiet and weightless as shadows. She knew that was the third team joining with the first already on deck somewhere, preparing for the attack. Soon, the signal would be called, and when that happened ….

A movement caught her eye, and she turned to see Kai once again by her side. He was looking down at her, an odd expression flicking across his face as he grabbed her hand, pressed it briefly, and then just as quickly leapt up the shrouds as fluidly as the others had. Once he reached where the shrouds met the mast, he crouched to his heels and signaled to Libby.

At the sight of his hand signal, Libby felt her breath rush from her lungs. She hiked her backpack tighter against her shoulders—it was heavier now as it bulged with small stones—then gulped in a mouthful of air, as if it might be the last she'd ever take.

And then, she began to climb.

Her legs shook so fiercely that at first she could barely lift one foot without her other losing its grip, but she tried to ignore the sensation and continued on. Halfway up the shrouds, she stopped and took her position, hooking her wobbly left leg and equally wobbly left arm through the rope netting to steady herself.

Below her, she could see inside the barricade where the sailors congregated, her eyes so adjusted to the darkness that the few lanterns within seemed to glow bright as bonfires.

She kept her eyes on the barricade as she reached for her slingshot tucked into her back shorts pocket. Then she dug out a little stone from the collection she'd poured in her two front pockets and placed it in the sling. Bumps trickled down her arms and legs as she waited, not daring to move her gaze from the barricade; not daring to even blink.

And then, she heard it:

A low caw came from above—Lofah's signal—and for a moment, there was utter silence, followed by a return call that must have come from a nearby seabird. Libby's ears pounded like marching band drums, her heart matching its beat as she raised her slingshot and took aim.

Just as her stone flew forward, a flurry of stones and bricks were hurled from her teammates above, down upon the pirates. A roar of flames erupted in the next second, and Libby realized a lantern within the barricade had been hit. Three of the pirates yelped and rushed to put out the fire while the others raised their guns and fired into the sky, still blind to the team's location. Far below from where Libby perched, the remaining freed prisoners scrambled over the deck, some climbing the barricade toward the forecastle where the pirates were located, some slipping around it to climb up the foremast, all of them lugging bricks and stones and chains, while a line of men formed from the hatch to mid deck, creating an assembly line for handing off supplies.

Libby quickly shot three more stones in rapid succession, hitting one pirate in the chest, effectively distracting him from peeping over the stacked sacks in the direction of a prisoner who was creeping up the sacks to further the attack. More guns fired madly into the night.

"Libby, it is time!" shouted Kai above the chaos.

Chapter 21

But she already knew it was.

What she didn't know was ... could she do it? All of the people above her: Kai, Lofah and the three others ... all of them were relying on her. They trusted her. They were presently swinging from ropes and masts in the midst of gunfire *because* of her.

But could she do it?

The explosion of gunfire was deafening against the former silence of the night. Libby glanced up, realizing her friends above where sitting targets, with nothing to protect them from the bullets except the darkness. Well, the darkness ... and her. She took another deep breath, forcing herself to calm down and focus.

"Just like before," she breathed, staring at the glint of guns reflecting from the barricade's lantern fire, ignoring her own fear and focusing instead on what had to be done.

"Libby! Laion is hit!" shouted Kai, referring to one of the boys. "You've got to hurry!"

"I'm trying!"

Stones and bricks zoomed from above her, crashing into the barricade while revolvers and rifles blasted blindly. She watched the guns, shutting everything else out, even Kai, taking deep breaths as she did so, in and out, in and out, and then ....

Everything slowed down.

And with it, the sound did as well. The roar of flames and shouts and blasts of gunfire still filled the night, but now, it sounded quite similar to an old recording played in slow motion, so that the noise was less sharp and more drawn out and also, in a strange way, more distant-sounding.

As it had been before with the rock-throwing women, Libby could see the bullets moving through the dark sky: silver capsules parting the air as if traveling through sand. And as she watched the bullets, she found she could move their direction ever so slightly with her eyes, as if she could push the air around them, like creating a water current in a pool. Soon, the bullets moved over and past her friends above her.

Libby shook herself as real time returned in a disconcerting whoosh, and had she not had her leg and arm hooked into the shrouds, the sensation would have knocked her backward. She clutched her slingshot tightly in her fist, not daring to let go, then turned her attention once again to the barricade below.

The fire now smoldered weakly; someone had used a sail to smother it out, it seemed, but whatever fire had been put out was replaced tenfold by the fire in the pirates' eyes.

They were raging mad, cursing and shouting as guns blasted a cacophony that rivaled Fourth of July fireworks. The smell of gunpowder mushroomed everywhere as more gunshots exploded, but by now, the barricade had been breached.

Through the plumes of smoke, Libby could spot the prisoners on the forecastle deck within the barricade, using chains against swords and guns, and above her, Lofah was shouting directions, but all she heard were foreign words, with their names called intermittently.

"Libby," shouted Kai, pointing at a prisoner climbing up the barricade where, unbeknownst to him, a pirate waited with his rifle, "the man on the far left!"

She raised her slingshot, now grabbing another stone and slipping it into the pouch. She took aim.

A deep, calm breath.

She released, flinging the stone through the air in a blurry line. A second later, the pirate staggered backward, clutching his

Chapter 21

right hand where the stone had hit, sending his rifle crashing to the ground.

"Excellent aim!" exclaimed Kai in astonishment.

Libby grinned as the prisoner she'd just guarded scrambled to the forecastle and grabbed the pirate's gun. But in the chaos all around, another sailor had managed to sneak away from the fray, sword in one hand and pistol in the other. Libby took aim again.

CRASH! The sailor's sword fell to the deck as a stone smashed into his forearm. He yelped and looked around, bewildered, giving Libby just enough time to send another. This one missed, pelting the foremast instead, barely avoiding a prisoner who was currently wrestling an exceptionally burly pirate.

Kai must have noticed, too, because another stone—much larger than the ones Libby used—flew from above her and crashed into the deck an inch from the burly pirate's face. Even though it didn't make contact, it distracted the pirate enough to give the prisoner an advantage, and in a matter of seconds, he had the pirate belly down, wrists and ankles tied with rope.

"Not bad yourself! How's Laion?" called Libby, shooting another stone at the sailor still holding the pistol. Again she missed, but barely.

"Just grazed him, I think," replied Kai as he hurled a brick.

She shot another. Missed again. She dug into her pockets; she only had two stones left, and then she'd have to take off her backpack to replenish her stock. She grabbed one and placed it in the sling. She took her time with her aim, steadying her breath.

BAM! The pistol fired as her stone made contact, and what happened next was a blur of bizarre events:

The sailor's gun flew into the air as he cursed in pain,

clutching an arm that Libby's pebble must have hit. And then, a rope far above him snapped in two—presumably because of the misdirected bullet—followed by a strange wooden-sounding groan. For a split second, the sailor looked in dismay above him, just as the spiked trap they'd hoisted up earlier came crashing to the deck.

The sound of splintering wood mixed with the sailor's howls, and Libby realized the trap must have landed on his foot. A moment later, a prisoner tackled the sailor from behind, sending him yowling to the deck floor as his arms and legs met the same fate as his comrade's.

"How in the heavens did you learn to shoot like that?" yelled Kai.

Libby laughed, surprising herself; she'd never known until that moment how exhilarating it was to successfully unarm blackbirding pirates.

"My Uncle Frank taught me, but I didn't think I'd be this good, either," she admitted, shouting over the mayhem. "Maybe my lucky aim has something to do with the witching hour, like that one guy said!"

She glanced up to see Kai shaking his head in astonishment. And something else, too. Something like ....

"Libby!" Kai suddenly yelled. "Watch out!"

Chapter 22

Atamai's Revenge

Libby's gaze whipped back to the barricade.

In the seconds she'd looked away, another sailor must have figured out the direction of all those annoying pebble attacks, because now, a rather scary-looking rifle barrel pointed directly at her.

"Uh oh," she gulped, but before the sound fully left her lips, a blast of gunfire threw her backward.

"Libby!" Kai screamed as down, down, down she went, tumbling head over heels as her ankles caught in the shrouds, then an arm, an ankle again ....

"Umph!"

She gasped for air, but her throat felt as if it had been glued shut. She gasped again, and this time, a sharp pain split through the center of her chest. Finally, she started to cough in great, rattling wheezes.

At least she could breathe now, and when she'd calmed down enough to look about, she saw Kai leaping down the shrouds, and it wasn't until then that she realized she was, once again, in someone's arms.

Only this time, it wasn't a stinky sailor; it was one of the freed captives working the assembly line near the hatch, and from the look on his face, Libby guessed he was just as surprised to have caught her as she was to have been caught.

"Thank you," she groaned, trying to lift her head so she could see what was happening. The attempt sent another shooting pain through her chest.

"Do not move," replied the man holding her. He spoke in broken English, but the sound of his voice caught her attention.

"You ... you were the one who warned us about the sailor Pierre waking up!" she wheezed, recognizing his voice. "I thought it was the other guy who warned us—Atamai—but it was you, wasn't it?"

The man nodded as he carried her to the other side of the mainmast and then lowered her to the deck, carefully placing her by a coil of ropes. Above her, she could see Lofah, Laion and the two other boys climbing down the shrouds, and from the shouts near the forecastle, she guessed the sailor with the gun had been overtaken ....

She looked back at the man. "What's your name?"

"Toa," he replied, concern shadowing his face.

"Libby, are you alright?" panted Kai, now hovering above her. "Can you breathe? Are you in pain?"

"I'm ... fine, I think," she said, once again craning her neck

Chapter 22

to see, but the effort made her feel as if she might crack in two. She fell back.

"It's my chest, right here." She lifted her arm and pointed to the center, and just as she did this, her finger brushed against a small hole in her t-shirt. She pushed against it, surprised, then felt a hard, flat surface underneath.

"The necklace!" she gasped, suddenly understanding why there was no blood. "I ... I think the bullet must have hit the amulet! It must have blocked it!"

Kai and Toa exchanged glances.

Carefully, Libby lifted her hand, now pinching the titanium chain between her thumb and index finger as she tugged it upward so the moonstone could slip through the neck of her t-shirt, but as soon as she pulled, it felt as if she were tugging a giant suction cup from her skin.

"I ... think I'd better leave it there for now."

She tried again to sit up, and this time, she was able to scoot into a half-sitting, half-lying position so the ropes propped up her back. As soon as she'd achieved this, she became aware of how quiet everything had become. The forecastle above the barricade was practically silent, with only a few moans coming from the tied-up pirates, and the freed captives, while obviously victorious in their attempt to overthrow the ship, stood mutely, their expressions a mix of confusion and anger.

Kai and Toa must have noticed the silence as well, each glancing to the mainmast above, where, moments before, Lofah, Laion and the other two boys were still descending. But now, they were nowhere to be seen.

Libby gulped as she followed their gaze.

"Where are they?" she whispered, a sick feeling creeping into her stomach.

As if by way of an answer, a familiar voice far to her left boomed, "Time to conduct a trade, gentlemen and ... sorceress!"

The sick feeling in her stomach tightened into a knot as Libby turned in the direction of the voice, ignoring the pain that still split through her chest, and saw what she was hoping against hope she wouldn't see:

Toward the stern of the ship, on the quarterdeck above the captain's cabin, stood Pierre, the sailor who was supposed to be shackled in the hold. And not only was he *not* shackled, he'd also regained possession of his pistol—an alarming enough fact—but more alarming was the fact that the pistol was currently aimed directly at someone.

And that someone ... was none other than Ginny.

Libby inhaled sharply, so horrified at finding Ginny held at gunpoint that it took another moment for her notice that Atamai—the freed prisoner who was supposed to be watching over the hold—stood on the main deck just below Pierre, with Laion and one of the other boys locked in chains to one side of him. To the other, a cannon pointed toward the forecastle, where most of the freed prisoners currently stood.

"Atamai!" cried Libby, hardly even aware of her own voice. "What are you *doing?*"

Atamai slid his gaze her way, and as their eyes met, she once again saw terrible scenes from his island home, just before he'd been taken prisoner by Captain Hayes. Then, just as quickly, the visions stopped.

"I am doing what needs to be done," he replied.

"Do not do attempt any witchery, or your friend will meet an untimely end," added Pierre from the quarterdeck, and as he spoke, he jabbed the pistol against Ginny's temple so hard that

Chapter 22

she trembled, tears trickling down her cheeks. "But if you cooperate, your friend will be released unharmed."

"What is it that you want?" demanded Kai in English, and at this, Pierre smiled.

"What *we* want, young man, is simply to have what is due us. If you had any sense in your head, you would have planned for the same."

"And what's that?" snapped Libby.

Pierre kept his gun pressed against Ginny's temple as he answered:

"We want to save our captain, of course; what good does it do to overthrow his ship? He will only hunt us all down and make us pay for our actions ten-fold. But if we return him to his rightful position, and if these men see the error of their ways, we will release your friend and these boys for good measure."

Atamai nodded in agreement. Then he turned to the captives who stood on the forecastle and began speaking to them in his native tongue.

Libby glanced at Kai. "What's he saying?"

Kai's jaw tightened as he listened, his brows drawing together. "He says he has tried in vain to lead them," he reported, his voice low. "At least eight of these men come from the same island as he, and though he is older and more learned than his brethren, he was scorned by them and humiliated when he attempted to organize a defense plan. He claims that he had predicted an invasion such as Captain Hayes's blackbirding years ago, but no one would listen to him. Instead, they ridiculed him for his paranoia and ostracized his family."

Kai paused, anger flashing in his eyes as he continued to listen to Atamai speak to the other prisoners. "So now, he says they should all accept their fate and start new lives in the plantations where they will be sold. He says they should be grateful to have another chance ...."

"Why is he saying all of this?" Libby demanded. "Wasn't he the one who said we should fight while there is something left to fight for?"

"I expect it was a ruse," replied Kai as the freed prisoners on the forecastle deck muttered angrily. "He must have known it would serve him no purpose to persuade them in the hold; he'd be overthrown in a trice, not to mention he may have been fearful of your powers. But now, he has the upper hand; he knows you dare not risk hurting your dearest friend."

Rage swept through Libby, and without even thinking about it, she rose to her feet, too angry to even notice the pain in her chest.

"And what about you, Atamai?" she shouted, her hands balling into fists. "Will you accept your fate? Will you be sold to a plantation as well?"

Atamai gave no answer, but Pierre laughed, for a moment taking the gun off Ginny's temple long enough to waggle it in the air.

"No, our clever friend Atamai made a deal with the devil some time ago. Poor fools, no one realized it was he who thwarted their last attempt to escape! Our Captain is no simpleton; he knows there is no better guard of prisoners than a prisoner himself. Who better to spy and report, to ensure matters do not get out of hand? And in return, our friend is promised great riches upon delivery of ...," Pierre paused to throw a sneer at the freed prisoners before finishing, "our *cargo.*"

"Why would you do that?" Libby yelled, turning from Pierre to Atamai. "Why would you betray your own people?"

Atamai's eyes were hard as steel.

Chapter 22

"I have no people," he retorted, his voice hollow and flat. "My family was murdered when I was captured. They died while attempting to protect me. If anyone had afforded me the respect due when I tried to warn them years ago, none of this would have happened."

"So now you'll turn these men into slaves, all because you're mad at them for not *listening* to you?"

Atamai shrugged. "I have given them more than one opportunity to heed my advice. It was their choice to scorn me. Every choice has a consequence and now, because of their arrogance, I have nothing more to live for while they face the outcome of their own doing. What do I care what happens to them? I might as well enjoy the comfort a little wealth provides for what time remains."

Libby swallowed hard, barely believing the words Atamai spoke. He was so cruel, so unfeeling, and the idea that this same man was the one who had suffered so much and felt so much—feelings she'd felt herself when she'd looked into his eyes—was impossible to reconcile.

"Enough talk!" bellowed Pierre from the quarterdeck, just as a seabird squawked from somewhere near the barricade. "Slaves, put down your weapons and untie my men, and no one will be harmed!"

Atamai repeated the command in his own tongue, gesturing to the cannon. As he spoke, Libby sensed Kai drawing closer to her.

"I think he will not hesitate to shoot if our men do not comply," warned Kai under his breath. "If they surrender, he has much to gain; if they do not, he has little to lose. Even if that cannon should sink this ship and take him with it, he knows he is a man whose soul is already dead."

Libby nodded numbly, realizing Kai was right. But what could she do? Even if she tried her slowing-down-bullets-trick with the cannon fire, Pierre's gun was pressed straight to Ginny's head; one split second, and her best friend could be dead. Libby didn't trust her magic enough to attempt stopping a bullet that close; it was far too risky.

She closed her eyes, racking her brain for any idea that might save them, but the only thing that came to mind was of Sir Jasper. She clenched her jaw impatiently, annoyed at herself for such a stupid thought. Even if she *could* communicate with Sir Jasper right now, what help could he possibly give?

But then, something else sprang to mind:

If she could communicate with rats, what else might she communicate with?

Admittedly, Sir Jasper and the rest of the ship *Rattus* were remarkably intelligent, so maybe the trick only worked on animals that read Shakespeare or something, but it still presented a possibility, didn't it? A possibility that something else might be able to come to their aid? She needed something unexpected; something that would distract Pierre or Atamai long enough to be overthrown; she needed the element of surprise ….

But how?

And more importantly, *what?*

She kept her eyes closed, trying to block out the million distracting thoughts racing through her mind. If she'd learned anything about herself in the last twenty-four hours, it was that she needed to pay more attention to what was already in front of her rather than what she wished was there. Isn't that how she'd discovered her slowing-down-rocks trick? And for that matter, how she'd discovered she could communicate with Sir Jasper?

She had to *listen.*

Chapter 22

Another squawk came from somewhere behind her, which only increased her agitation. It reminded her of the giant albatross that had landed on the *Liberté*, and *that* made her think of Uncle Frank and Sal, who were probably pacing the deck at this very moment, worried sick. And worse, if Pierre and Atamai were successful in their efforts, she knew they'd be coming for the *Liberté* next, and when that happened ….

A tremor ran through her as her mind flashed through a zillion possibilities, all of them horrible. And each negative thought produced another, until she found herself racing from one worry to the next: about her sick mom, about the broken time machine, about poor Ginny trembling at gunpoint, about all the terrible, hopeless things that she had no idea how to fix, especially not now. Without even realizing it, that strange nausea in her head took over again, growing stronger with each horrendous prospect.

Libby squeezed her eyes shut harder, forcing the racing thoughts away. It was her mind. She wouldn't let hopelessness control her. She could *do* something. She took a deep breath.

Listen.

That's the first step.

Just listen.

A rush of wings whooshed behind her, followed by a loud, distinctive, "Honk!"

Libby's eyes flew open. Then she almost fell backward into the pile of ropes as a bird zoomed past. She caught her breath in amazement, her eyes glued to the bird that wasn't a seabird at all ….

No, it was a large, white *goose*, now flying straight for Pierre.

Chapter 23

The Promise

If Libby had hoped for something unexpected, then she definitely got it, because there isn't much else *less* expected in the world than seeing one's pet goose attacking a South Seas pirate.

The seconds that followed were a mass of confusion.

Before Libby could shout a warning, Pierre lifted his gun toward Buttercup, took aim and fired.

"NO!" she screamed, but even before the words came out, she realized Pierre was screaming, too, and that the bullet he'd just shot had completely missed Buttercup. Instead, Pierre was now hopping on one foot, then another, roaring profanities as Buttercup swept around him, honking madly and nipping anything he could with his bill.

Then she realized what must have happened: Ginny must have kicked Pierre in the shins as soon as he'd lifted his gun

Chapter 23

away from her, because she was still kicking him as if he were a human soccer ball, left shin, then right, left then right, shouting random things with each furious kick, such as:

"That's for pointing a gun at me!" and "That's for making fun of my freckles!" and "That's for being a horrible person!"

Meanwhile, Atamai remained at the cannon, but now, Libby could see him reaching for a gun he'd tucked into the waistline of his pants. He was too late, though, because now Laion and the other boy Atamai had captured were swinging the chains binding their wrists like whips, battering Atamai's torso and arms while several of the freed prisoners on the forecastle deck grabbed guns from the tied-up sailors. Before Atamai realized it, several guns were pointed in his direction while five men charged toward him.

Lickety-split, Libby shrugged the backpack from her shoulders and grabbed a handful of stones out of it, slipping one into her slingshot as Buttercup continued his attack of Pierre from above and Ginny continued to kick and scream, both of them keeping the sailor so distracted that he'd forgotten all about the gun in his hand.

"I'll shoot, you get his gun!" she shouted to Kai, but Kai was already on his way, charging up the quarterdeck with a speed that would have totally impressed her if she hadn't been so distracted.

It was hard enough aiming at a thrashing, howling target, but what really worried her was the possibility of hitting Ginny or Buttercup in the process. She took aim at Pierre's chest, figuring it would be too high up to hit her best friend and too far down to hit her pet.

A deep breath. Focus.

And then...

THWACK!

Pierre sputtered, clutching his chest where Libby's stone had hit it. She placed another in her sling, just in case, but by now, Kai had reached the quarterdeck. Between Ginny's kicking and Buttercup's nipping and Libby's on-target shot, Pierre hadn't noticed the cabin boy coming up to him.

Libby held her slingshot as she watched, her pulse jumping wildly as Kai hurtled toward the pirate and tackled him to the ground. The gun must have spun from Pierre's grasp in the process, because the next thing Libby saw was Ginny scrambling for something on the deck. Suddenly, Ginny was brandishing the gun, then pointing it with trembling hands toward Pierre.

"Surrender!" she bellowed amid the hubbub, but Ginny's voice was so shaky that even she looked unconvinced.

Thankfully, several of the freed prisoners had joined Kai on the quarterdeck and were now cinching a rope around Pierre's wrists as they pulled him to his feet.

Libby turned to check on Atamai, hardly believing how well everything was going—especially considering her horrible luck in the past twenty-four hours—and saw two freed prisoners dragging him toward the hatch, presumably to shackle him down below. Even in the dark, Libby could see that his eyes were hollow, without any emotion, not even despair, and for a split second, she felt sorry for him.

She remembered the scenes she'd seen through his eyes, how he'd lost his family; how he'd witnessed the death of his wife and sons. The pain he'd felt was so great. Was it possible that something like that could kill a man? Maybe not physically, but kill the good inside?

She didn't know, but as Atamai was lowered through the hatch, she gulped down the knot in her throat, then turned

Chapter 23

away. She couldn't fix what was wrong with him. She knew that, but still, it made her consider people in a different way; to consider evil in a different way. It wasn't as black and white as it once seemed. It didn't make it right, what Atamai did, but in a way, she could almost understand ….

She shuddered, but then glanced over at her friends standing on the quarterdeck, and a feeling of utter joy swept through her.

In the next moment, she was running toward them (well, closer to limping, really, as the ache in her chest still hurt awfully), passing a cursing Pierre, who was being dragged to the hatch by two other men. When she reached the ladder leading to the quarterdeck above, her friends were already tumbling down it—a good thing, since she wasn't sure if she could climb just yet—and then she was throwing her arms around Ginny, then Buttercup and then, before she'd even realized what she was doing, around Kai.

"Ah, young love," drawled Ginny.

This immediately brought Libby to her senses. She drew back and lowered her arms, embarrassed. Kai appeared equally flummoxed, and for a painful minute, they just stood there, avoiding eye contact.

"Oh, relax. I'm just teasing. It's obvious you can't stand each other."

"Stop it," muttered Libby.

Kai gave her a small smile and touched her arm. "You were very brave out there," he said, ignoring Ginny. "You know what we spoke of earlier? Whatever darkness you sense you have, I have seen what you are made of. You are brave and kind and loyal. And you have a strength about you that can outmatch the battles within, I am sure of it."

Libby swallowed, hardly knowing what to say. And her

cheeks burned so hot she worried they might glow in the dark. "You were pretty awesome yourself," she stammered shyly.

"Oh, barf," said Ginny.

"What? You were awesome, too!" she protested, turning to her best friend. "I've never seen you kick like that!"

Ginny grinned. "I had a lot of pent-up anger toward that guy. But you know what? If we ever get back home, I think I just might try out for the soccer team …."

Libby laughed and Buttercup honked loudly, as if in agreement.

"And *you* were amazing!" she said, scooping Buttercup into her arms. She turned to Ginny. "I think Buttercup can hear my thoughts! I mean, I can't talk to him like Sir Jasper or anything, but I think he knew what needed to be done …."

"Speaking of whom," interjected an annoyed, high-pitched voice, and Libby turned to see the form of Sir Jasper stepping from behind the ladder, not two feet away. He stood on his hind feet, clasping what must be the world's tiniest ledger in his right paw as he continued.

"While we applaud your victory, we do hold you indebted for our services." He cleared his throat and opened the ledger, raising an eyebrow as he did so. Minute font filled the tiny pages, and Libby wondered how anyone could write—much less read—such microscopic script.

"To wit," Sir Jasper continued after a moment of consulting his document, "we have chewed unsavory rope, sustained unnatural levels of activity, risked our very lives *and* spied upon pirates, the latter being exceptionally nerve-racking for those of us suffering from an irrational fear of eye patches." He paused for effect. "Ergo, wherefore and thusly, we expect delivery of that which is due us henceforth!"

Chapter 23

Ginny scrunched her nose, whipping her head around as her eyes searched the quarter deck. "I heard that! Was that the ... *Rattuses?* They want their peanut butter, don't they?!"

Libby laughed.

"A promise is a promise," she replied, winking at Sir Jasper. Then she turned to Ginny with a grin. "And we've got a jar of golden treasure to deliver ASAP!"

Chapter 24

The Severed Curse

The wind remained still as they rowed through the darkness, and with each stroke of the paddle, the sky slowly shed its velvet curtain. Soon, Libby knew it would be dawn.

A new beginning.

But what sort of beginning would it be?

For Kai and his shipmates, they would finally return to their homes: some to that cupcake island they'd sailed past, some to farther-flung lands. For Captain Hayes and his crew of blackbirding pirates, well, as soon as they were delivered to the *Leonora*, their fate would be decided by the freed prisoners. But what about the rest? Even though she had the moonstone amulet back in her possession, would it be enough to fix things?

Questions spun through Libby's mind like sticky webs.

She sighed and rubbed her face, suddenly realizing how

Chapter 24

exhausted she was. She guessed she should be since it was hours past midnight; probably close to five in the morning. Between the time they'd overthrown the bad guys and now, there had been a lot of discussion back and forth—specifically about how to best deliver peanut butter and the four sailors on board the *Liberté*—but absolutely no sleep.

Given the lack of wind, they'd all agreed that the easiest way to conduct their exchange was to paddle to the *Liberté*, then use the diesel engine to move closer to the *Leonora,* though it took Libby and Ginny a while to explain to everyone what exactly a diesel engine *was*.

She shook her head, trying to shake out the tangle of thoughts, then looked around. Kai rowed in the front of the boat while Lofah rowed in the back; they'd insisted on doing this, especially since the center of Libby's chest still hurt from the amulet's impact, making it difficult for her to row. Ginny sat beside her in the middle, and while her best friend maintained a relentless commentary on Kai's paddling technique—intermixed with vivid descriptions of Uncle Frank's inventions aboard the *Liberté*—Libby hadn't said a word since they'd lowered themselves into the rowboat.

"If they think the diesel engine's amazing, I can't wait until they meet Esmerelda," whispered Ginny with a wicked grin.

Libby nodded, but she wasn't able to match Ginny's mood. She didn't know what was wrong with her. She should be excited. Elated, even. Other than *not* finding a radio, she and Ginny had succeeded in their mission, hadn't they? The prisoners were now free; the bad guys locked up. So why did she feel so confused?

Maybe because we're still stuck in the 1800s, she considered darkly. *Maybe because my mom and dad are still out there, almost*

150 years away, and if we don't get back to them soon, who knows what will happen? And maybe because I've got this thing inside of me that's growing stronger ....

"You're thinking about The Incident, aren't you?" guessed Ginny, halting her paddling critique long enough to notice Libby's worried expression.

"Yeah," admitted Libby. "Among other things."

Ginny pursed her lips.

"Well," she said after a moment, "I never got to finish what I was trying to say before; about your mom, remember?"

Libby nodded again, pushing loose strands of hair from her face, then she glanced over at Kai. He sat facing them as he paddled, his own face drawn in thought. Even though she had no doubt he could hear every word of their conversation, somehow, she didn't mind him listening.

"It all goes back to what Sabine told you before," continued Ginny, "about how everyone in the coven is connected. Zelna is part of the coven. So are you; so's your mom. But *I'm* not."

"Okay," agreed Libby, not quite following.

"So, just like Sabine said, when you confronted Zelna in the cave, you touched *evil* ... evil that doesn't affect me in the same way because I'm not connected to it. But it changed *you*. Even before The Incident, you've been different ... because Zelna—something that is pure evil—*touched* you. So you're right; ever since the cave, your mom has been intercepting Zelna's power to protect you. But since you've been away from *her*, it's gotten worse for *you*. You said it yourself. You're fighting whatever's inside you now without your mother's help!"

"And during The Incident?" asked Libby uneasily. "The ... thing you saw?"

Chapter 24

Ginny gripped the wooden bench under her with both hands, her eyes growing wide at the memory.

"Well," she eventually replied, "I think maybe it's like how those fragments from the other two stones suddenly combined with your amulet. Those stones exploded with Zelna; they should be gone, right? But during The Incident, all that blue light came back …." She stopped and glanced at her friend.

"It wasn't just the stones that came back," Libby acknowledged, finishing Ginny's thought. "I could feel *her* power, too. Whatever had exploded with those stones—that part of Zelna must have come back as well."

"Exactly. So that means you're fighting *more* of her now!"

Libby chewed her bottom lip, struggling to process all that Ginny had just said.

"So … I'm taking on the full-strength version of Zelna now; is that what you're saying? That the same thing that's making my mom sick is now totally on me?"

"I think so! And you must be super strong to not even be a little sick or anything …."

"But I *do* feel sick," Libby confessed. "And right before The Incident, that dizzy-nauseated feeling kind of grew until it felt like it was everywhere—"

"But your mom, she had a white streak in her hair that very night in the cave," interjected Ginny, "right after she shouted those words, remember? And since then, she's gotten sicker and sicker. So if you're taking on Zelna by yourself now, you should at least be showing a few more symptoms than your behind-the-eye dizzy thing, right?"

Libby puffed at a strand of hair sticking to her face. It was light brown, just as it had always been, with no sign of white. "I guess you're right," she admitted.

"So maybe that's part of your powers. Zelna said it herself: that your biggest strength is your goodness, remember? Well, she considered it a weakness, but still, if you're supposed to be a super-witch, maybe you're using the strength of your goodness to fight Zelna's evil!"

Libby swallowed hard. It was a lot to process, but the horror of The Incident couldn't be denied. She shuddered at the memory, the darkness of it scratching at her mind, as if a jar of spiders had been opened, releasing its inhabitants all over her in a scuttling, black wave with no way to brush them off; as if she could feel *evil* creeping over her skin and through her nose and into her mouth, even her eyes, until those crawling, dark things became a part of her, joining with the remembrance of those terrible chants, of what Ginny saw, of what Libby *felt* ....

Yes, Zelna had come for her.

For a brief, terrible moment, she'd even succeeded in taking *over* her ....

"What I'm trying to say," continued Ginny, "is that you're strong enough to fight Zelna. Even if it's hard, you can do it; I *saw* you do it!"

Libby rubbed her arms as she blinked back at Ginny, that heavy, nightmare-like sensation still lingering. It seemed impossible that so much darkness could be within her; it was too terrible to be real. How could she have that and remain who she was?

Because despite what Ginny said, she didn't *feel* strong. Or particularly *good*. How could she fight such a power? There wasn't exactly a guide book on How-to-Battle-An-Evil-Witch-Soul inside of you. And now, she didn't have her mom—the one person who might know what to do—to ask about it. In fact, it would be impossible for her mother to be further from her ....

The swirl of gloom in Libby's mind suddenly froze, and in

Chapter 24

its place, a sliver of light appeared, like a laser beam of hope, melting away the shadows.

"So ... if you're right," Libby said, thinking it through as that sense of hope bloomed larger inside, "then Mom *can't* protect me now—I'm too far away from her. Right? And if that's the case," continued Libby, "then *that* means she must be doing better!" She laughed at the realization, now feeling so relieved she felt as if she could float straight into the sky. "I mean, she doesn't even have a choice in the matter! She's been *forced* to stop protecting me!"

"Well, I hadn't thought about it like that," admitted Ginny, "but it makes sense, sure." She shifted on her bench, then glanced at Kai as he pulled at the oars. "And why is this taking so long?"

"Would you care to offer your assistance?" he muttered in reply.

Libby laughed again, suddenly feeling as if the weight of an entire humpback whale had been thrown off her shoulders. Maybe they were still stuck in the late 1800s, and maybe Zelna really was a part of her now, but her mother would be okay. Their separation had severed whatever curse it was that drained away her mom's life, and just knowing that gave Libby the strength to face whatever came next.

She looked at Kai. "Trust me," she said, feeling so giddy with relief that she couldn't stop grinning. "I've tried that suggestion on Ginny before, and it's a definite no-go. She's more of a ... director kind of person."

"Anyway," added Ginny with a humph, propping her feet up on a coil of rope, "you'll be rowing your Captain Hayes and the feathered pirates back to the brig, so you might as well get some practice." She ignored Kai's glare and turned back to Libby. "Speaking of villains, I wasn't done with my theory."

"We are all of us bursting with anticipation," said Kai.

"Well, it's just that Libby's freaked out, right? I mean, *I* sure would be if I had evil witch particles inside of me. But I've been thinking that over, too …."

"How fortunate for us."

Ginny flicked her right hand in the air. "It's like art class, you know?" she persisted, as if dismissing Kai's presence. "When Ms. Fisher taught us to use shadows to create depth and contours, to make something look three-dimensional. But in life, it's the opposite. Life's already three-dimensional."

"Considering what Uncle Frank's machine has done," said Libby, gesturing to the ocean around them, then at Kai and Lofah, "I'd say there might be a few more dimensions than that!"

"Whatever. My point is, that in *real* life, it's not the shadows that create depth, it's depth that creates the shadows." She paused for a moment, as if struggling to find the right words. "I mean, take a cave, for example. It's not darkness that creates a cave; it's the cave's depth that creates the darkness—the space inside that goes so deep that light can't reach it …." As her voice trailed off, she frowned. "I'm not making any sense, am I?"

"On the contrary," declared Kai, "that is the first sensible thing you have uttered all night."

Libby raised her hands in mock dismay. "So, basically, you guys are saying I'm like a cave? Thanks."

Kai shook his head. "It is the things that happen to us that create our depth," he explained, still pulling at the oars. "The more depth a person has, the more darkness they have as well; it is unavoidable. But perhaps it also makes the light in them that much brighter …."

Chapter 24

"What *I'm* saying," interrupted Ginny with another glare Kai's way, "is that now, you've got another side to you—you've got *more* to you than most. But you can choose what you do with it, right?"

"Such as choosing to be completely unhelpful when your comrades are doing all the work," suggested Kai.

"Oh, she's helping," said Libby. "You've no *idea* how hard it would be if Ginny weren't here to tell you what to do!"

Kai snorted at that, but then he caught Libby's eye, and soon, they were both snickering.

Ginny looked at them in disgust. "Well, I hate to break up the *hilarity,* but we're here."

And sure enough, when Libby glanced up, she saw the *Liberté* floating before them, highlighted from behind by the faint glow of dawn rising from the sea. She could hardly believe it. But in case she had any doubt, there was Esmerelda peering over the side, waving her arms and shouting:

"About-time-Liberty-Frye! What-took-you-so-long?"

Chapter 25

Paradise Found

After answering a gazillion questions from everyone, Libby managed to pry off the moonstone (she now had a strange, circular imprint in the center of her chest that she suspected might be permanent) to show Uncle Frank. His eyes widened at the transformed shape, a low whistle escaping from his lips.

"Phenomenal!"

"Do you think it can fix things?" Libby asked eagerly. "I mean, if this stone interacted with my own weird powers to send us here, don't you think it could send us back? Especially now that the amulets are all … er, combined?"

Uncle Frank didn't respond. He just sat there staring at her necklace for a good five minutes, deep in thought, his eyes almost as wide as the moonstone. Then, without a word of explanation, he clicked over to the cabin door and disappeared

Chapter 25

downstairs for another thirty minutes before rejoining them on deck.

"Apologies for the cryptic behavior," he eventually replied, "but I didn't want to say anything until I'd checked with my journal. A few thousand pages takes some time to sort through!"

"But what about the machine? Can you fix it?" pressed Libby impatiently.

"Oh, that." Uncle Frank glanced toward the cabin, as if just now considering the possibility. "Let me see ... well, I do have enough tools on board to work on the machine, but I don't have all the supplies. And, to be honest, even if I *could* fix it, I wouldn't know how to reverse what's been done. It's a bit like Russian roulette, Libby."

"What do you mean?"

Uncle Frank lifted his hands, palms up, then let them drop. "I mean it is a terribly dangerous game of chance. Maybe the machine could send us back, or maybe you'd end up five centuries away and me in another. There's no way to anticipate what might happen. I learned my lesson last time; you were right to be angry at me before. And it would be foolhardy to attempt anything further without a better grasp on how this works—"

"So ... we're stuck here?" Ginny interrupted, her voice growing panicked. "I just had rats crawl all over me for *nothing?*"

"Well, there is one other option; it's what I was looking into downstairs." Uncle Frank glanced again at Libby's stone, amazement still in his eyes. "I'd like some more time to think things over before I say anything more on the matter, however ...."

"Perfect," said Libby, glancing over the sea to where the *Leonora* floated in the distance. "Because we've got an invitation to a luau this afternoon. You can think away there to your heart's content!"

Ginny's frown spread into a wide grin. "Yeah!" she added with renewed enthusiasm. "And this time, they *promised* us there would be absolutely no stone-throwing involved!"

Palm trees swayed overhead, fronds grasping at the sky with long, leafy fingers that made soothing, rustling sounds.

The sweet, honeysuckle-like scent of frangipanis wafted in the air, combined with a hint of smoke from a kitchen fire. Beyond the outdoor kitchen, Libby could see the underground, earthen oven where a pig was being roasted in the traditional island way. Kai had explained that the oven was called an *umu*, and that it was fueled by stones heated in a fire, then placed inside the oven. In a few more hours, the pig would be perfectly cooked from the heat of these stones and would serve as the centerpiece for their celebration feast.

Libby glanced from the *umu* to Uncle Frank, who chatted with a group of men nearby. They sat in a circle, each taking turns sipping a murky beverage called *kava* out of a coconut shell. A young woman sat in the center of the circle with a *kava* bowl, and each time the coconut shell emptied, she'd refill it, then hand it back to Uncle Frank.

"Tastes like black pepper and dirt!" Libby heard Uncle Frank remarking between sips. "And my gums are going a little numb …."

His comments were drowned out by the high-pitched chattering mixed with euphoric sighs behind her. Libby grinned and turned around. "Good stuff, right?" she asked, watching the group of *Rattus*.

They sat in their own little kava circle of sorts, except instead of a *kava* bowl, a plastic jar of peanut butter stood in the center.

"It is indeed gllllorious!" cried Sir Jasper, who had peanut

Chapter 25

butter stuck to his whiskers, and probably to the roof of his mouth as well.

"Crunchy and smooth at the same time, like the pop of an ant on one's tongue!" agreed another.

"Like a perfectly decomposed snail ... only sweet!" added a third as he licked his paws.

Libby tried not to wrinkle her nose. She muttered some excuse to politely leave them to their business, then walked over to Sal. He sat below an ironwood tree, his back to the wide, twisted trunk and his bald head covered with a hat made from woven pandan leaves. A banana leaf filled with chopped papaya and bananas rested in his lap.

"What did I tell you?" said Ginny, joining them. She wore a wreath made of woven flowers and glossy, green leaves around her neck, and her arms, legs and face shone clean and bright from a coconut oil scrub she'd just had at the nearby spring. Flopping onto a woven mat that lay on the ground beside Sal, she pronounced, "This place *is* a resort after all!"

Libby laughed. "I guess it is."

"More like paradise!" corrected Sal, dropping another slice of papaya into his mouth. Libby had lost count of how much fruit Sal had eaten, but she knew he couldn't possibly still be hungry. It didn't stop him. Sal smacked down banana leaf after banana leaf of the stuff, then grinned widely as a beautiful woman came to bring him more. "This is the life," he resumed with sigh. "Too bad we have to leave in the morning."

The idea sent a pang through Libby's chest.

But she knew Sal was right. According to Uncle Frank, they should have headed out already—they had a *lot* of ocean to cover—but the freed prisoners had insisted they join them for a feast on the cupcake-like island before parting ways.

The three younger boys and seven of the men were all from there, so Kai's crew had agreed to hand Captain Hayes and his band of pirates over to the island chief for judgment. As for Atamai, he would be returned to his island home, where a tribunal there would decide his fate.

Libby wondered what would become of the pirates; did they have prisons like they did back home? And if so, was there a chance Hayes would ever get released on account of good behavior?

She thought about that as she walked toward a bluff that looked out over the ocean. From here, she could see both the *Leonora* and the *Liberté* anchored beyond the turquoise ring of outer reefs. She spotted a dinghy and several canoes going back and forth, where supplies were being loaded onto both ships for their respective journeys.

Not only had the freed captives insisted on sharing at least half of the *Leonora's* cargo with the crew of the *Liberté*, but the islanders were bringing supplies, too. Soon, they'd have more dried bananas and mangos and woven baskets filled with taro root and bread fruit than they'd know what to do with. And while Libby couldn't see her, she knew Esmerelda watched with her infrared vision from the *Liberté's* cabin, keeping a record of it all … and probably creating a two-month dietary plan in the process. Buttercup had stayed on board as well, just in case something happened to Esmerelda and they needed to be alerted. Uncle Frank had agreed this was the wisest decision.

"We are tampering with history enough as it is," he'd declared. "The last thing we should do is introduce a robot to island dwellers in 1871!"

"Care to see something amazing?"

Libby jumped at the sound, then turned to see Kai standing

Chapter 25

beside her. He'd managed to leave the *kava* circle, and when she looked in its direction, she understood why. Uncle Frank and his new group of friends were now enjoying an afternoon nap. While he was zonked out in his mobile unit (which was in wheelchair mode), the others lay on woven mats spread over the ground.

She glanced from Uncle Frank to Ginny, but her best friend was sacked out on her woven mat as well, sleeping contentedly under the shade of the ironwood tree.

Libby, however, couldn't sleep.

Even though she was way past tired, she had too many questions running through her head that just wouldn't shut down ….

She forced her attention back to Kai. "Considering all that's just happened," she said, attempting a smile, "I think I've already seen a *lot* of amazing."

"But this is different; this is something you have to … jump into, so to speak."

That caught her attention.

Kai's dark eyes twinkled. Then he turned and said, "Follow me!"

Fifteen minutes later, they stood on a small, sandy shore. To their right, rocks climbed one on top of the other, creating a wall that reached into the water. Behind them, cliffs rose to the sky, pocked by little caves that served as homes to the birds darting to and fro. Even from here, Libby could hear the birds' bell-like trilling, their songs combining with other birds chirping from tree tops, their bright wings flicking in the sun.

She still couldn't believe how beautiful everything was. The island was so green, the water so blue, the colorful tangle of flowers and fruit trees and palms so dazzling that it felt like something fabricated for a Disney movie or something. But the sand under her feet and the breeze on her face assured her all was real.

"Do you trust me?"

Libby dropped the hand she'd used to shield her eyes from the sun and peered up at Kai. She made a face.

"Kind of late to be asking that question, don't you think? Like, probably pre-pirate-mutiny late?"

"Ah!" retorted Kai, raising an eyebrow. "Modern humor. I shall take that as an agreement upon the matter. In any case, fortune smiles upon you today; it is low tide, so it will make things much easier!"

Before she could reply to that, he trotted over to the rise of rocks on the right side of the beach, climbed on top, then disappeared over the other side with a splash.

Libby scrambled after him, and when she reached the pinnacle of rocks, she saw Kai treading water below, where a sink hole formed a natural swimming pool that glimmered jewel-green in the sunlight.

"What is the delay? Jump!" he cried.

Libby glanced from Kai to the rocks under her feet.

"I'm from Mississippi!" she called, half laughing, half hiding her hesitation. "We don't *have* cliffs over beautiful blue water! And anyway, I'm scared of sharks!"

Kai threw back his head and laughed, sending drops of water spinning through the air like diamonds.

"The outer reef protects us largely from such a thing. Come, Libby. It is well worth it!"

It did look like fun ….

Libby jumped, shouting something like "Ahggg!" until she

hit the water. Warm liquid enveloped her, and for a few seconds, the world fell silent.

"Not bad," Kai chuckled as she sputtered to the surface, "but this is where the adventure begins. Take a deep breath, Libby. You will need to hold it until we resurface. And open your eyes once you are under water; it will only sting but a trifling. Very well?"

"Wait. What do you mean by ... *trifling?*"

Kai just grinned.

"Inhale!" he said, then he took her hand and disappeared once more under water, tugging her with him.

Chapter 26

Where Time Begins

Sunlight danced through the water, sending strange contours over coral and craggy rocks.

Orange and yellow and ruby-red fish darted before her eyes, while a school of tiny, turquoise ones swarmed in cloud-formation, then disappeared just as quickly, like translucent gemstones spilled from the sky. Libby stared at it all in wonder, feeling as if she were swimming inside a giant aquarium.

In front of her, through the crystal-clear water, she could see a rough-hewn opening in a wall of rock. The opening dazzled bright blue, highlighted from within by mysterious shafts of light.

Kai swam through it and Libby followed, her heart thrumming giddily. She rose with Kai to the surface on the other side,

Chapter 26

where light shone so brightly through the rippling water that she had to squeeze her eyes shut from the glare.

She felt the sea slide from her skin, her face feeling the cool air. Libby gulped in a deep breath, then opened her eyes to look around. She blinked rapidly from the slight sting.

"Over here!"

She turned in the direction of Kai's voice, and saw him swimming to a natural, rocky step rising from the water. He was already sitting there by the time she reached it.

Libby crawled onto the step, ran the palms of her hands over her eyes, then looked around.

"Whoa."

"Is that a twenty-first-century expression for amazing?"

Libby nodded, numb with awe. She'd never seen anything like it.

All around them, limestone walls climbed at least a hundred feet high, where, far above, deep green vines crawled down the ledges. Libby and Kai were completely surrounded by these walls, but directly above, a wide opening let in the sun, made all the more dazzling by the light glancing off water. The water, in turn, glowed an electric, powder blue.

"It is a sacred grotto," said Kai, answering Libby's unspoken question. His voice rang eerily against the limestone. "I read of this place from a journal my teacher obtained years ago. It was left by another traveler, who spoke of a legend someone once told him, along with instructions on how to reach this place. After reading about it, I have always yearned to visit, but earlier today was the first opportunity I have ever had. Once I saw it, I knew I should share it with you."

"Thank you," said Libby, but her voice came out in a whisper.

Water lapped, then echoed against the limestone walls, creating a rhythmic, mystical sound as if they were inside a magic well, surrounded by rocks and forest. She half wondered if she could swim to another world in that powder blue water before her. Or maybe, she considered, they were already *in* it ....

"I am pleased to know you like it," replied Kai teasingly. "Would you care to hear the legend?"

Libby nodded again. She couldn't take her eyes off the water.

"The story goes that, long, long ago, when time first began, the great god Maui fished these islands from the sea. He used a magical fish hook, pulling up one isle after the next. When he pulled up this island, he was so moved by the beauty of his toils that a tear escaped from his eye. When it fell to the ground, it pierced the stones straight down to the sea. The pool before us is what is left of Maui's teardrop, mixed with the tides and rain."

"That's ... beautiful," said Libby.

"Yes, it is," agreed Kai. "This place, though it represents a legend of how our earth began, remains untouched by the passage of time. Some day in the future ... let us say over 150 years from now, I venture that it will still look largely the same." He stopped and peered over at her, a shy smile twitching at his mouth. "Perhaps, someday, long after I am gone but you remain a young woman, you will return here and think of me."

Libby tore her eyes from the water and met his gaze, swallowing down the sudden tightness in her throat. "I'll *never* forget you, Kai." It came out in a single, rushed breath. "I've never met anyone like you. I wish ...." She stopped, unable to finish, because how do you say goodbye to a person whom you've just trusted with your life? Someone who's trusted theirs to you? How do you leave someone like that behind? Forever? Without even a chance to write or call? No way to keep in touch?

Chapter 26

She didn't know how, but even if she did, she knew it still wouldn't smooth away the ache in her chest.

"And what about you?" she eventually asked instead, forcing the tremor from her voice. She quickly rubbed her hands over her eyes, pretending to wipe away the sea. "When will you return to your home?"

Kai squinted as he looked up into the sky. "I shall sail with the others tomorrow. The men from this island shall join as well, and return with the ship when the rest of us are reunited with our families. We will first deliver the traitor Atamai to his homeland—as well as the other men who hail from there. And then we shall set sail for my isle." He paused and glanced over at her.

"I wish you had the time to visit my family there," he added with another shy smile, "but I understand your journey is a pressing one."

"I wish I could, too," she agreed wholeheartedly. "But Uncle Frank says there's no time to waste; he almost didn't agree to this feast—Ginny and I had to beg him! He says it could take us two months to get to wherever it is he's planning …."

"Two months is a long time to be on a ship. I speak from experience."

Libby twisted her mouth as she looked back at him. "You sure you don't want to come with us? Even for a little while? I bet with all of your sailing around, you've never actually done it just for *fun.*"

Kai threw her a knowing glance. "I have my brethren here, just as you have your own to return to. Beyond that," he continued, giving her a playful jab in the ribs with his elbow, "when you are successfully returned to your time, what shall I do then? I should die from shock at seeing you suddenly disappear … or however this strange phenomenon of space-time travel works."

Libby laughed, despite the knot in her gut.

"Hey, you could ask Uncle Frank to transport you with us!" she suggested hopefully. "Whatever he has planned, I can't imagine it's got to be any harder to transport another person. You could go to school and then college. My parents would totally help you out—you'd love them. And you could stay with Uncle Frank and Sal! Then you'd end up being a famous scientist or something—I know you would!"

Kai shook his head, his eyes again serious. "How would I cope in this future of yours? I should be constantly vexed and beside myself in confusion. No, Libby, I am certain your world is too fast for me."

Even though Kai spoke kindly, his words fell like icicles on her skin. She crossed her arms, fighting the panic in her chest.

"What if we never make it back to our time, though?" she blurted, and as soon as she said it, she couldn't stop herself. "What if Uncle Frank's grand plan doesn't work out? I mean, whatever it is he's thinking of, it's got to be pretty far-fetched."

"You mean the idea that I am presently conversing with someone who has traveled from another century ... or the idea that you will somehow find a way to return to your home?"

Libby puffed out her cheeks, then exhaled slowly. "When you put it like that, I guess it doesn't sound any crazier than what we've already been through," she admitted. "And Uncle Frank says he thinks he knows exactly where we need to go, so maybe there's hope after all ...."

"There is almost always hope, if we do not give into despair."

Libby snickered. "You sound like a fortune cookie!"

"I do not know this 'cookie of fortune' of which you speak ...," Kai began with a frown, but this response only made Libby snicker more.

Chapter 26

"Ah!" he said, his eyes alight with understanding. "Once again, you mock my speech!"

"I dost?" she replied, widening her eyes and shaking her head innocently. "Nay, good sir! Nay!"

A reluctant smile tugged at Kai's mouth. "By the by," he said after another moment, "you sound rather ridiculous to me as well."

The wind lashed ropes against masts, making strange *tonging* sounds. Gulls cawed overhead. The air smelled sharp, like salt and metal, whipping its way through clothes and hair, pushing against skin.

Libby watched as the anchor of the *Liberté* rose from the water.

"All set!" called Sal from his position by the mainmast.

Uncle Frank flicked a switch, killing a motor that ran the anchor pulley, then pulled a lever to raise the sails. He looked up from his panel of controls as steam hissed through metal valves.

"Ready, Libby?" he asked, his eyes gentle. Even so, he couldn't disguise the eagerness dancing underneath them.

"Of course we're ready!" said Ginny. She jumped to the tip of the bow, then waved both arms at the people in the canoes below.

"Malo 'aupito" she cried giddily, reciting the Tongan phrase for 'thank you' she'd learned. "*Malo 'aupito* for the wonderful feast and for all of our supplies! *Malo 'aupito* for the spa treatment, too! That coconut stuff is amazing! And *malo 'aupito* for the ...."

The groan of sails rising up masts temporarily drowned out the rest of Ginny's farewell. The white, trapezoid and triangular sheets fluttered, then ballooned in the wind, tugging the *Liberté* from the jewel-like reef. Ginny was still calling out her goodbyes as the reef inched away from them. All the while, Libby stood speechless, watching Kai, who stood waving from the deck of the *Leonora*.

They never did say goodbye.

She waved back, not caring that tears leaked from her eyes. Instead, she smiled. "Thank you," she whispered.

Kai's face blurred with her tears as she saw him smile in return. She never dropped her gaze as the wind pushed them farther and farther away from that cupcake island in the distance, away from the jewel ring of reefs. Away from the *Leonora*.

Away from Kai.

The wind tugged harder at the sails. Tears splashed the wooden deck by Libby's feet. And then, Kai and his ship were nothing but a white blur on the horizon.

Buttercup honked loudly, then made a strange, trilling noise. Libby turned to see him ruffling his wings at an albatross that had landed on deck. She wondered if it was the same one from before.

"Better enjoy the company while you can, bud," Sal harrumphed. "Cause where we're going, the only bird you're gonna see is a perfectly cooked Peking duck!"

"Stop-that!" exclaimed Esmerelda. She crossed her arms and then did something weird with her metal eyebrows.

Sal waved a hand. "Aw, just teasing, Essie. Can't that robot brain of yours understand a joke by now?"

"It-does-when-I-actually-hear-something-funny!"

Uncle Frank raised his eyes to the sky and muttered, "This is going to be a *long* journey."

Libby was just about to agree with him when Ginny joined them at the wheel. "So where exactly are we going again?"

Chapter 26

Uncle Frank instantly cheered at the question. He squinted over the sea, his eyes bright with anticipation. "We're headed for the port of Qingdao, China—just a bit north of Shanghai!"

"And that's where this wizard guy lives, right? Qin ...." Ginny stopped and made a face. "How do you pronounce it again?"

"Cheeng-dow," answered Uncle Frank. "And technically, the wizard Sheng lives *near* there, on a mountain top. It's where the Emperor Qin traveled to meet him all those years ago when searching for eternal life ...."

"Right!" declared Ginny, cutting him off. "Creepy emperor who built the secret city that runs off the energy of Libby's moonstone. Simple. We just go to this mountain, hand the stone over to the wizard so he can do his thing for the ghost emperor, then get blasted back to our time, right?"

Uncle Frank chuckled. "That's one way to put it." He paused, then glanced at Libby, his eyes once again thoughtful. "So I guess we're off to see the wizard!"

The sound of those words sent tingles over Libby's arms, straight down into her fingertips. She looked around her, and even though she'd just lived through the strangest two days of her life, she couldn't help but question if it all had actually happened. Or, for that matter, if *this* was happening: a sailing voyage to nineteenth-century China in order to find some magical, time-space-traveling wizard.

It sounded crazy.

The sails billowed and popped overhead, tugging like horses eager to race. She wondered if there was a bit of magic in them as well. It seemed like there was magic in everything lately.

Like the fact that her mom was going to be okay. Or even the beauty of that cupcake island they'd left behind, or of the amazing creatures she'd seen: the magnificence of the humpback whales, the peculiar visiting albatross or the fish that fly from water to air ....

Weren't all those things magical, too?

A pang went through her chest at a sudden memory of a smile and a warm laugh and dark eyes that dazzled—all belonging to a friend whom she'd never see again. Libby crossed her arms and turned to face the sea. The wind whipped at her hair and stole tears from her eyes, sending them trickling backward over her temples. She didn't mind. She closed her eyes and breathed in the air so filled with energy that it, too, felt magical, as if it danced inside of her, becoming something else, becoming something *more* ....

Ginny and Kai's conversation from earlier about how darkness is just life's way of creating depth, of creating more of you, echoed in her mind. And somehow, suddenly, to Libby, the magic that was in her didn't seem quite as scary anymore.

Even the darkness.

She took another deep breath, the salty air swelling within her with a sense of hope. She knew they still had so much to do before they could go home. And even though only two days had passed in their current time, she missed her mom and dad terribly. But the thought that, somehow, this journey had also saved her mother's life made everything else worth it.

"Kiddo, you alright?"

Libby turned to see Uncle Frank watching her, concern shadowing his face. His springy, brown and silver hair twisted in the wind, his long-sleeve shirt billowing like a parachute, and that energy she'd felt in the air seemed to materialize in his face, in those alert, inquisitive eyes that never grew old.

She glanced from Uncle Frank to Esmerelda and Sal, who

Chapter 26

were still bickering, then to Buttercup. He honked as the albatross lifted its wings to the lashing wind, then flew away. Ginny ran over to watch.

"That is so dangerous!" she exclaimed, shaking her head in disapproval at the disappearing seabird. "That air current is far too strong; he should have waited!"

Libby smiled and turned back to her Uncle Frank, remembering how happy she'd been when she first saw him yesterday when they'd returned on the rowboat. How she'd climbed up that rope ladder despite the pain in her chest, then hugged him, her throat too tight with tears to speak. How suddenly, she had felt that everything was going to be okay.

"Yeah," she said, meeting his gaze. "I'm great."

And she meant it.

Because even though being back together on the *Liberté* wasn't the same as being home, it was the next best thing in the whole wide world.

THE END

About The Author

J.L. McCreedy first learned a love of writing (and developed an incurable condition of wanderlust) while growing up in Southeast Asia as the child of missionaries. She holds a B.A. in English and a law degree, freelances as a writer and consultant for charitable organizations and, whenever possible, drags her splendid husband across the globe on ill-planned, shoestring adventures.

Visit her at www.TongaTime.com

Made in the USA
Lexington, KY
23 February 2017